Handbook of
Procedures and Functions
for the
BBC Micro

Other Granada books for BBC Micro users

Introducing the BBC Micro
Ian Sinclair
0 246 12146 7

The BBC Micro: An Expert Guide
Mike James
0 246 12014 2

Discovering BBC Micro Machine Code
A. P. Stephenson
0 246 12160 2

Advanced Machine Code Techniques for the BBC Micro
A. P. Stephenson and D. J. Stephenson
0 246 12227 7

Word Processing for Beginners
Susan Curran
0 246 12353 2

BBC Micro Graphics and Sound
Steve Money
0 246 12156 4

6502 Machine Code for Humans
Alan Tootill and David Barrow
0 246 12076 2

Practical Programs for the BBC Micro
Owen Bishop and Audrey Bishop
0 246 12405 9

21 Games for the BBC Micro
Mike James, S. M. Gee and Kay Ewbank
0 246 12103 3

Disk Systems for the BBC Micro
Ian Sinclair
0 246 12325 7

Learning is Fun –
40 Educational Games for the BBC Micro
Vince Apps
0 246 12317 6

Advanced Programming for the BBC Micro
Mike James and S. M. Gee
0 246 12158 0

Take Off with the Electron and BBC Micro
Audrey Bishop and Owen Bishop
0 246 12356 7

Handbook of Procedures and Functions for the BBC Micro

Audrey Bishop

and

Owen Bishop

GRANADA
London Toronto Sydney New York

Granada Technical Books
Granada Publishing Ltd
8 Grafton Street, London W1X 3LA

First published in Great Britain by
Granada Publishing 1984

Distributed in the United States of America
by Sheridan House, Inc.

British Library Cataloguing in Publication Data
Bishop, Audrey
   Handbook of procedures and functions for the BBC Micro.
   1. Microcomputer
   I. Title   II. Bishop, O. N.
   001.64′2   QA76.8.B35

ISBN 0-246-12415-6

Typeset by V & M Graphics Ltd, Aylesbury, Bucks
Printed and bound in Great Britain by
Mackays of Chatham, Kent

Contents

Preface   vii

Notes for readers in the USA   ix

Introduction   1

Section 1: Procedures

     Procedures and how they work   9

     The Procedures   16

Section 2: Functions

     Functions and how they work   101

     The Functions   104

Locator table   140

Preface

All of the procedures, functions and calling programs in this book were written and tested on the Model B BBC Microcomputer running BASIC II under Operating System 1.2. We believe that almost all, if not all, of the programs will also work equally well on BBC machines with other operating systems or with BASIC I.

In a book of this kind and size, the decisions on what to include or omit necessarily reflect the interests and preferences of the authors. We have picked out those routines which we personally find to be most useful in programming the BBC Micro and we hope that you will find them useful too.

We would like to thank Daniel Bishop for helpful advice and assistance during the preparation of this book.

Audrey Bishop
Owen Bishop

Notes for readers in the USA

The American and UK versions of the BBC Microcomputer differ in the number of screen lines and in the number of pixels in the vertical direction. This makes it necessary to alter a few of the procedures, or to limit the input values of Y within a smaller range than that specified in the text. The routines concerned and the alterations required are given below.

PROCanimate: Input Y between 0 and 24.
PROCborder: Alter line 170 to:

   170   VDU 31,0,18,CB

PROCbox: Input Y between 0 and 17.
PROCcircle: Input Y between 0 and 799 (try 400).
PROCdelete: The screen will not hold two lists of ten items each, with headings. In lines 10 and 40, alter the '10' to '8', so that only 8 entries are required for the list.
PROCdoubleheight: Input Y between 0 and 19.
PROCexplode: Input Y between 50 and 749.
PROCmoveacross: Input Y between 0 and 24.
PROCmovedown: Input Y between 0 and 21.
PROCpolygon: Input Y between 0 and 799.
PROCrectangle: Input Y between 0 and 799.
PROCsideways: In Modes 0,1,2,4 and 5, input Y between 0 and 25; in Modes 3 and 6, input Y between 0 and 22.
PROCsolidpolygon: Input Y between 0 and 799.
PROCsolidrectangle: Input Y between 0 and 799.
PROCtelescreen: Alter lines 150 and 190 to:

     150   FOR Y=0 TO 17
     190   VDU 28,3,19,39,0

FNlimit: Limit Y between 0 and 24 in Mode 4.

FNvaliddate: To adapt this function to the American format for dates, MMDDYY, alter the variable *month* in line 140 to *day* and alter the variable *day* in line 150 to *month*.

Introduction

When a certain operation has to be repeated several times during the course of a program, it is convenient to write it as a procedure, a function or a subroutine. These routines are also useful in allowing us to write programs that let us see clearly what the program is doing.

The first part of such a program is an easy-to-follow outline calling upon each procedure, function or subroutine to do its work when required. The second part consists of the definitions of the procedures and functions used and the subroutines. These may then be called on from different points in the remainder of the program by using the appropriate BASIC keyword. In this way all three are similar. In most other ways, and certainly in all important ways, they are very different.

We are not concerned with subroutines in this book, since BBC BASIC provides us with procedures and functions which are faster and altogether more powerful than subroutines. So the next point to consider is the difference between a procedure and a function. When should we use one and when should we use the other?

Putting it in the simplest possible way, a procedure is a way of *doing* something. If you want the computer to display a coloured border around the edge of the screen, use a procedure. If you want to move a picture of a horse from one side of the screen to the other, a procedure can be written to do this. If you want the user to type in a response to a question, a procedure can ask the question and ensure that the user types in an acceptable response.

In general, a procedure says to the computer 'Do this!' These examples explain the essence of procedures but, as might be expected, there is much more to be said on this subject. For more details, see the beginning of Section 1, *Procedures and how they work*.

A function also 'does something', but in a much more restricted sense. In essence, a function has a *value* and for this reason a function is used in a BASIC statement as if it was a variable. Its value depends on the nature of the function. BBC BASIC has many functions already defined, so we can take a few of these as examples. The function SQR performs the operation of calculating the square root of a number. For instance, we can write a program line such as,

    X = SQR (A)

in which the value of the function SQR is the square root of the value of the variable or expression in the brackets. If *A* is 81, for example, the value of *SQR (A)* is 9. In the statement above, this value is assigned to the variable *X*. Alternatively, we might write:

    PRINT SQR (A)

The computer then prints the value of *SQR (A)*, which is the square root of the value of *A*.

   Some functions operate on strings. A familiar example is LEFT$, which requires two values in the brackets. The first value is the value of the string which is to be operated on; the second is the value of the variable which decides how many characters are to be taken from the string to become the value of the function. For example, we could write:

    X$ = LEFT$ (A$,B)

If the value of *A$* is "MICRO" and the value of *B* is 3, the value of LEFT$ (A$,B) is "MIC". In the statement above, the value of the function is assigned to X$. We could instead use the function in statements such as PRINT LEFT$(A$,B), and INSTR(LEFT$ (A$,B),"C").

   The BBC Micro has many useful functions included in its BASIC but, inevitably, the program we are writing will need a function which has not been provided. Fortunately, as will be explained at the beginning of Section 2, *Functions and how they work*, the Micro also allows us to define our own functions.

● Summing up:
     Procedures *do*
     Functions have *values*

How to use this book

The book is divided into two main sections. The first contains all the procedures, the other contains all the functions. Procedures and functions are so diverse in their nature and in their applications that it is simplest to arrange them by name, in alphabetical order. If you can remember the name of a procedure and function that you have used before, you will be able to find it straight away by looking in the appropriate section.

To help you find a new procedure or function to perform a given task, we have devised a *locator table*. Possibly you may not be certain whether it is a procedure that you are looking for or a function, so the table lists both together. The table indicates the application or applications of each procedure or function, so you will quickly be able to find the one you need. For ease of reference, the locator table is placed at the very end of the book.

Another use for this book is as an introduction to programming. Each program, consisting of the calling program with the procedure or function, is a short, self-contained program. These programs are easy to understand and clearly explained. Beginners may learn much about BASIC by experimenting with the input and modifying the programs.

Procedures and functions cannot be used on their own. They need to be called or used by a program, such as the calling program referred to above. We have designed the calling programs to help you discover what the procedures and functions can do. Most of our calling programs ask you to key in various values, so that you can experiment with the procedures and functions, finding out how they behave under different conditions, and how to control or use them effectively. When you have tried them out and want to use one or more of them in a program of your own, there is no need to base your program closely on the design of our calling program. Take each procedure or function as a separate and independent unit and incorporate it in your own program. The way to link its action to that of your program is described later.

Saving procedures and functions on tape or disk

Building up a collection of procedures and functions on tape or disk is a good way of saving programming time. It also reduces the occurrence of typing errors. You can buy a tape or disk holding all the procedures and functions in this book (see notice at the front of the book). If you prefer to build up your own collection, use the following sequence of operations.

Begin by making a list of the routines you intend to save. Working with each procedure or function in turn, copy it from the listings given in this book (*omitting* the lines of the calling program and the row of asterisks on the REM lines). Renumber it, using the RENUMBER command, so that it does not have the same program lines as any other procedure or function in your collection, or line numbers that you are likely to be using in your main programs. Then save it on disk or tape, under a suitable file name. Keep a list of the file names, ready for referring to in the future.

Loading procedures and functions

Whenever you want to use procedures or functions in a program which you are writing, it is a simple matter to load them so that they become appended to the end of your program. The way to do this is as follows:

1) You need to have each procedure or function saved separately on tape or disk, with non-overlapping line numbers, as explained above. Alternatively, they may be saved in groups, as described below.

2) Load the program which you are writing. It may be the whole of the program or just a part of it – maybe it consists of only the first line, for example '10 REM ** MY PROGRAM **'.

3) Type 'END', then press RETURN.

4) Then type PRINT ~TOP-2, and press RETURN. A number is displayed which is the starting address at which the procedure or function is to be loaded. This number is a four-digit hexadecimal number.

5) Type '*LOAD "NAME" HHHH' and press RETURN. (Note the '*' before the 'LOAD'.) In the example above "NAME" is the file name of the procedure or function you are loading. HHHH is the four-digit hexadecimal number you obtained at stage 4. Check the number very carefully, making sure that you have typed it correctly, *then* press RETURN. If you are using a disk drive, the procedure or function will be loaded automatically. If you are using a tape recorder, the usual 'RECORD then RETURN' message will appear; position the tape and load the file in the ordinary way.

6) If you list the program now, you will find that the procedure or function has been added to the end of it. You can repeat stages 3 to 5 as many times as you like, so collecting together all the procedures and functions needed for your program. If you are loading several routines in this way, take special care at stage 5. Remember to type the '*' before 'LOAD'. If you leave out the '*', the computer simply loads the latest routine, replacing everything you have put together so far. The same thing happens if you forget to key in the hexadecimal number before pressing RETURN.

Saving groups of routines

It is usually more convenient to save your collection of procedures and functions in groups rather than singly. Routines that always need one another can be typed in together and saved as one file. For example, a program which uses PROCdoke will generally need FNdeek as well. It makes sense to save these two together as a group. From then on, only a single operation is needed to load them. Procedures such as PROCcircle, PROCrectangle and PROCpolygon are likely to be needed in the same kind of program so these three (and possibly others) may be saved under one file name. After you have loaded such a file into your own program, delete any routine which you do not need.

The technique of saving associated procedures and functions in groups is adopted in the special tape and disk mentioned at the beginning of the book. The routines are saved as 30 groups, any one of which can be loaded by keying in the group number.

Grouping routines has an additional advantage for disk users. The number of files on a disk is limited to 31, so it is wasteful of disk space to load short routines. Saving routines in convenient groups of 2 or 3 makes it possible to include all of the routines in the book on a single disk.

Section 1
Procedures

Procedures and how they work

The program lines which define a procedure begin with a statement which gives the procedure its individual name. It is usual to type the name in lower-case letters, and this must follow immediately after the defining keywords DEF PROC.

We use the keyword ENDPROC to indicate the end of the definition. The general form of the definition of the procedure thus becomes:

```
500 DEF PROCname
510 REM This is where
520 REM the program lines
530 REM tell the computer
540 REM what to DO
550 ENDPROC
```

Note that DEF PROC is *two* keywords, while ENDPROC is *one* word.

When we want the computer to perform the action of the procedure we 'call' the procedure, using its name. We can do this from any point in the program by using the keyword PROC:

```
20 PROCname
30 REM the next line of the program
```

Line 20 above sends the computer to the procedure to do whatever is required. The computer works its way through the program lines of the procedure. When it reaches the word ENDPROC, it returns to the line following the line which called it – in this example, line 30.

A procedure may be called as many times as we like during the running of a program and may also be called from a line in another procedure. A few examples in this book even show a procedure calling itself.

Usually, though not necessarily, the name of a procedure which is being defined is followed by a list of one or more variables, enclosed in brackets. These are known as the *parameters* of the procedure. Parameters are values which control the action of the procedure. For example, PROCwait (described in more detail later in this section) has two parameters. The definition of PROCwait begins like this:

    80 DEF PROCwait (K$,T)

The two parameters are a string variable $K\$$ and a real variable T. The action of PROCwait is to make the computer wait until the user has pressed a specified key, or until a given length of time has elapsed. The value of $K\$$ is the character of the key which is to be pressed. The value of T is the maximum length of the delay, in hundredths of a second. These two values are required by the procedure in order that the computer will know what key to wait for and how long to wait. If $K\$$ has the value "W" and T has the value 0, the computer waits in the procedure until key 'W' has been pressed before continuing with the main program. On the other hand, if $K\$$ has the value "" and T has the value 300, it waits for *any* key to be pressed or until 3 seconds have passed. This is what is meant when we say that the parameters control the operation of the procedure.

    The next point to consider is how the parameters are given the values referred to above. There are several ways of doing this. The simplest is to place the values in brackets after the name of the procedure when it is called. For example:

    40 PROCwait ("Q",0)

The values "Q" and 0 then pass to the procedure giving $K\$$ the value "Q" and T the value 0. Each time the procedure is called we can use a different pair of values if we wish. Note that if the procedure is defined with a list of parameters following its name, you must always include the list of values after its name when calling it. The two lists must have the same number of items and the types of variables must 'match'. In the example above, both lists have two items, the first being a string variable and the second being a real variable. Integer variables may also be used as parameters.

    Instead of using values such as "Q" and 0 as parameters when calling a procedure, we may use variables or expressions. It would be of more general use to call PROCwait like this:

    40 PROCwait (response$,period)

If the program has previously assigned the value "Q" to *response$* and the value zero to *period* this statement has the same effect as the call given earlier. Similarly, we could use a call such as:

40 PROCwait (LEFT$(answer$,1),B+200)

Here we have two *expressions* as parameters. If, for example, *answer$* had the value "QUIT" and *B* had the value −200, this too would produce the same result as the call listed earlier.

The description above shows that if a procedure has parameters, they are of two distinct kinds. The parameters which are quoted in the definition of the procedure are known as the *formal parameters*. These are the variables which are to be used by the program lines within the definition of the procedure. When we call the procedure we quote another set of parameters known as the *actual parameters*.

The formal parameters are decided on once and for all when we define the procedure. The actual parameters may, if we wish, be different every time the procedure is called – not only in value but also in the way they are expressed in the calling statement. On different lines of the same program we might call PROCwait using values on one occasion, using variables on another occasion and using expressions on a third occasion. Any or all of these different methods of stating the actual parameters may be used, as convenient, at different parts of the program.

In our calling programs we have always used named variables as the actual parameters. The choice of names for these variables is usually the result of the design of the calling program. However, when you use the procedures in your own programs there is no need to use our variable names as actual parameters. You can use the names that suit the program you are writing. Or, of course, you can call the procedures using numeric or string values as parameters, or using expressions as parameters, in the manner described above. Provided that the list of actual parameters used when calling the procedure exactly corresponds to the number and type (integer, real, or string) of parameters listed in the definition of the procedure, the procedure will be properly linked to your program and can be called from it.

● To sum up:
Formal parameters: used in defining a procedure; must be variables.

Actual parameters: used in calling a procedure; may be values, variables, or expressions. (The term 'expressions' also includes functions, such as SQR(X) or functions that we have defined ourselves.)

One further possibility is that an actual parameter can have the same name as the corresponding formal parameter. For example we could call PROCwait by using a line such as:

```
40 PROCwait (response$,period)
```

These actual parameters will have been given values before PROCwait is called. PROCwait works as expected, but an interesting fact emerges which is best demonstrated by an example:

```
 10 N=99
 20 PRINT "First  ";N
 30 PROCdisplay(N)
 40 PRINT "Fourth ";N
 50 END
 60 REM ****************************
 70 DEF PROCdisplay(N)
 80 PRINT "Second ";N
 90 N=N*2
100 PRINT "Third ";N
110 ENDPROC
```

The program above consists of two parts, the main program (lines 10 to 50) and the definition of the procedure (lines 70 to 110). Note the use of the keyword END at the end of the main program. This is to prevent the computer from continuing on to the procedure after it has finished running the main program. It is essential to terminate the main program properly, as above, otherwise an error condition is certain to occur. The line of asterisks is not essential – it is put there just to make it easier for you to see where the main program ends and the procedure begins.

When this program is run the value of N is displayed four times, once before the procedure is called, twice during the procedure itself (before and after doubling it) and finally after the return to the main program. Line 10 gives N the value 99 which is displayed by line 20. Then the procedure is called. The procedure displays this value, then doubles it to 198 and displays it, just to prove that it has done so. But, on return to the main program we find that N still has the value 99! The explanation is that the N used in the main program (or calling program) is not the same as the formal parameter N used in the procedure. They have the same *name* (N) but they are different variables. Changing the value of N in the procedure does not alter the value of the N of the main program. We say that the N used in the procedure is a *local variable*. Any variable used in the definition of a procedure as a formal parameter is automatically made local.

One advantage of this is that you can use the procedures given in this book without having to worry about whether the variables used as formal parameters have the same names as variables that you are already using in your main program. Your own variables will remain completely unaffected by any operations on variables within the procedure.

Frequently we need to use variables in procedures that are not listed among the formal parameters. An example is when a procedure includes a FOR...NEXT loop. A variable such as *J* might be used as the loop index (loop counter). The same variable name might also be used for the same purpose (or for other purposes) in the main program. But calling a procedure which has *J* as a local variable will not alter the value of the *J* of the main program. It is even possible to have a program such as this:

```
10 FOR J=1 TO 5
20    PRINT "Main"J
30    PROCloop
40    NEXT
50 END
60 REM ************************
70 DEF PROCloop
80 LOCAL J
90 FOR J=101 TO 103
100    PRINT "Proc"J
110    NEXT
120 ENDPROC
```

The two *J*s are incremented independently and the loops operate without mutual interference.

In this example, it is obviously not appropriate to declare *J* as a formal parameter, since no value is to be passed to it from the main program. Instead, it is described as a local variable in line 80. One or more variable names can be declared as a list in such a statement. It is advantageous to declare all the variable names used in a procedure as local variables, either by listing them as formal parameters or by including them in a LOCAL statement. This prevents any possiblity of interference with the main program.

Sometimes it is necessary to return the value of the variables to the main program. Then the procedure uses a variable which originates in the main program and which is *not* defined in the procedure as a formal parameter. (Naturally it must not be included in a LOCAL statement either.) Such a variable is called a *global variable*. It retains its value whether in the main program or in the procedure. On the whole we prefer to avoid this. As explained above, there is the risk of using the same names in procedures as may have already been used in the main program. However, there must be an exception in the case of arrays since there is no method for passing a whole array as a parameter or for defining a local array. In other words, all arrays are global.

However, an *element* of an array (not a whole array) can be used as a parameter, either actual or formal. Thus we can call PROCwait in yet another fashion, using the elements of arrays:

    40 PROCwait (response$(3),period(N))

The arrays *response*$() and *period*() will have already been dimensioned and filled with values in the main program. The procedure may also be defined using the elements of these arrays:

    80 DEF PROCwait (response$(3),period(N))

This leads to the curious result that the array *response*$() has an element, *response*$(3), which has one value in the main program, but may be given an entirely different local value within the procedure. The same applies to *period*().

Describing the procedures

In the section of the book which follows, each procedure is described under the following headings:

What it does: a brief description of its action.

Formal parameters: a list of the variables, in order of appearance in the procedure, and a description of how they are used.

Local variables: a list of the variables and how they are used.

Actual parameters: a list of the values, variables or expressions, used in *our* calling program.

Global arrays: a list of these (if any) and how they are used.

Listing: this is in two parts – an example of a calling program, followed by the procedure. The listing has a line of asterisks to make it easier to distinguish one part from the other.

How it works: a description of the operation of the procedure.

Calling program: a brief description of how to use this. The calling program is intended to show you how to call the procedure when you use it in your own programs. It is normally designed so that you can feed a range of values to the procedure and find out what result is obtained. The procedures can be used in any mode, unless otherwise stated.

Variations: ways to modify the procedure to make it perform in other ways.

Associated routines: cross references to other procedures and functions which have actions related to that of the procedure.

The Procedures

PROCanimate

What it does: Displays an animated graphics character at any required position on the screen.

Formal parameters: *R*, the number of times the animation sequence is to be repeated.

    X, Y, the TAB coordinates of the position on which the character is to be displayed.

    C, the ASCII code of the first of the pair of user-defined characters.

Local variables: *J* and *T*, the loop indices.

Actual parameters: *repeats, tabx, taby, code*.

Listing:

```
10 MODE 4
20 INPUT "Enter the code, 224 to 254
"code
30 VDU 23,code,196,71,69,127,124,124,
72,108
40 VDU 23,(code+1),101,71,66,127,124,
124,72,108
50 INPUT "Enter the X coordinate "tab
x
60 INPUT "Enter the Y coordinate "tab
y
70 INPUT "Enter the number of repeats
"repeats
80 PROCanimate(repeats,tabx,taby,code
)
90 END
```

```
100 REM ***************************
110 DEF PROCanimate(R,X,Y,C)
120 CLS
130 LOCAL J,T
140 FOR J=1 TO R
150    PRINT TAB(X,Y)CHR$(C);
160    FOR T=1 TO 1000:NEXT
170    PRINT TAB(X,Y)CHR$(C+1);
180    FOR T=1 TO 1000:NEXT
190    NEXT
200 ENDPROC
```

How it works: The procedure displays a pair of user-defined characters alternately at the same location on the screen. This produces the illusion of movement. The characters will have been defined previously (in the calling program). The action of the procedure takes place in a loop (lines 140 to 190) which is repeated *R* times. At each repetition, the first of the two characters is displayed, followed by a pause (line 160). Then this character is replaced in the same position by the second character. A second pause follows, and the loop is then repeated.

When the procedure ends, the second character is left on display.

Calling program: This procedure works in any graphics mode. Mode 4 is used for this demonstration. You are first asked to enter the ASCII code for which you required the first of the two characters to be defined. The second character will be defined for the code number following this. Lines 30 and 40 then define two characters using VDU 23 statements. The characters given in this example program show a dog turning its head and wagging its tail.

Next you are asked to enter the two TAB coordinates at which the dog is to be displayed. X should be between 0 and 39, and Y should be between 0 and 31. Suitable values are 20 and 15 which place the dog at the centre of the screen. Line 80 calls the procedure, which clears the screen and displays the dog in action.

At the end of the procedure, the second character is left on the screen. In your own program you may want to remove it, either by printing a space at the same TAB position, or by clearing the whole screen. Or perhaps you may prefer to leave it there, motionless, ready to be animated again at some later stage in the program.

Variations: There is no end to the variety of graphics designs that can be used with this procedure. In any single program you could use up to 15 different pairs of characters, displayed at different parts of the screen.

If you wish to make the character move faster or slower, alter the 1000s in lines 160 and 180 accordingly.

Associated routines: PROCmoveacross, PROCmovedown.

PROCblankline

What it does: Clears the whole of the screen line that the cursor is on, returning the cursor to the beginning of that line.

Formal parameters: None.

Local variables: X, the number of characters per screen line in the current mode.

Actual parameters: None.

Listing:

```
 10 CLS
 20 INPUT "TEXT "text$
 30 PROCblankline
 40 END
 50 REM ************************
 60 DEF PROCblankline
 70 LOCAL X
 80 X=(?&352+256*?&353)/?&34F
 90 VDU 13,11
100 PRINT STRING$(X," ")
110 VDU 11,11
120 ENDPROC
```

How it works: Line 80 finds X by reading two values from memory. The first of these is the number of bytes needed for storing one screen line. The second is the number of bytes needed for storing one character. Dividing one value by the other gives X, the number of characters in a screen line. Line 90 is a VDU statement which sends the cursor back to the beginning of the line it is on and then sends it up one line. This is because it is assumed that, since the user will normally have just pressed RETURN, or the program will have ended with a PRINT statement with an automatic line-feed, the cursor will actually be on the line *below* the one that is to be cleared (see Variations, below).

The cursor is now at the beginning of the line which is to be blanked. Program line 100 prints a row of *X* spaces, so blanking out the line. This operation takes the cursor down to the beginning of the next line. Program line 110 moves the cursor back to the line which has just been blanked.

Calling program: You are asked to type in some text. Type in one, two or three lines, then press RETURN. Immediately the line the cursor is on is blanked and you will see the cursor at the beginning of that line. This procedure is useful for blanking out an incorrect response made to an INPUT statement. The cursor returns to the same line so that the INPUT statement and the typing of a response can be repeated. No matter how many times it is repeated, only one screen line is used and the format of the screen display is not destroyed.

Variations: If you are *not* using RETURN or a PRINT statement with an automatic line-feed immediately before this procedure is called, delete the comma and the '11' from line 90.

If you intend to use this procedure on a dual processor system, substitute this line for line 80:

    80   X = FNvdudeek (&52)/FNvdupeek (&4F)

Include FNvdudeek and FNvdupeek in the calling program.

PROCborder

What it does: Creates patterned, coloured borders at the top and bottom of the Mode 7 screen.

Formal parameters: *CT*, colour code for top border.
   T, ASCII code for Teletext character for top border.
   CB, colour code for bottom border.
   B, ASCII code for Teletext character for bottom border.

Local variables: *X*, loop index for X coordinates at which graphics blocks are displayed.

Actual parameters: *colourt, designtop, colourb, designbottom.*

Listing:

```
10 MODE 7
20 INPUT "ENTER ASCII CODE FOR CHARAC
TER "designtop
30 INPUT "ENTER ASCII CODE FOR CHARAC
TER "designbottom
40 INPUT "ENTER ASCII CODE FOR TOP CO
LOUR "colourt
50 INPUT "ENTER ASCII CODE FOR BOTTOM
 COLOUR "colourb
60 CLS
70 PROCborder(colourt,designtop,colou
rb,designbottom)
80 END
90 REM *************************
100 DEF PROCborder(CT,T,CB,B)
110 LOCAL X
120 VDU CT
130 FOR X=1 TO 38
140    VDU T
150    NEXT
160 VDU T AND 181
170 VDU 31,0,23,CB
180 FOR X=1 TO 38
190    VDU B
200    NEXT
210 VDU B AND 181
220 ENDPROC
```

How it works: Line 120 sets the control code for the colour of the top border. Then 38 of the chosen graphics blocks are displayed on the top line of the screen, forming the border. If, as is very likely, the chosen block is asymmetrical, the right end of this row of blocks will not be symmetrical with the left end. To overcome this problem, line 160 ANDs the value of *T* with 181. The effect of this is to find the code for a graphics block, the left side of which is the same as the left side of the chosen design, but with the right side blank. This design is displayed at the right end of the border.

The routine for displaying the bottom border is very similar. Line 170 moves the cursor to the bottom of the screen and sets the colour for

for the bottom border. Lines 180 to 200 display the border. Line 210 finds a suitable design to end the border and displays it.

Calling program: You are first asked to key in codes for the designs of the borders. Pick suitable designs from the chart of Teletext Graphics Characters, given in the Appendix to the User Guide. Suitable values are 178, 182 or 185, though you can use any in the ranges 160 to 191 and 224 to 254. Next key in the graphics colour codes in the range 145 to 151. You can, of course use the same designs and colours for both borders, if you prefer. The screen is then cleared and the procedure creates the borders.

PROCbox

What it does: Displays a title or other text surrounded by a box, in any colour.

Formal parameters: *X* and *Y*, the TAB coordinates of the top left corner of the box.
   C, the colour of the box and title.
   T$, the title.

Local variables: *J*, the loop index.

Actual parameters: *tabx, taby, colour, title$.*

Listing:

```
 10 MODE 7
 20 INPUT "Enter the title "title$
 30 INPUT "Enter the ASCII code for th
e colour "colour
 40 INPUT "Enter the X coordinate "tab
x
 50 INPUT "Enter the Y coordinate "tab
y
 60 PROCbox(tabx,taby,colour,title$)
 70 PRINT
 80 END
 90 REM ************************
100 DEF PROCbox(X,Y,C,T$)
```

```
110 CLS
120 LOCAL J
130 VDU 31,X,Y,C,183
140 FOR J=1 TO LEN(T$):VDU 163:NEXT
150 VDU 235
160 VDU 31,X,Y+1,C,181
170 PRINT T$;
180 VDU 234
190 VDU 31,X,Y+2,C,117
200 FOR J=1 TO LEN(T$):VDU 240:NEXT
210 VDU 250
220 ENDPROC
```

How it works: Line 130 has a VDU 31 statement to take the cursor to the position at which the top left corner of the box is to be drawn. The value of C sets the colour and, since it is in the range 145 to 151, causes Teletext graphics shapes to be displayed instead of lower-case letters. The shape displayed by code 183 is an inverted 'L', forming the top left corner of the box. The loop in line 140 then displays a row of blocks with coloured upper strips to make a horizontal band, forming the top of the box. The number of blocks is related to the length of the title. Line 150 then displays a shape to form the top right corner.

The cursor is moved down one screen line by the VDU 31 statement of line 160, which restates the colour code and then displays one block (code 181) to form the left side of the box. The coloured strip runs down the left-hand side of the character, so leaving a gap between the block and the title, which is displayed next (line 170). The semicolon at the end of line 170 keeps the cursor on the same screen line, ready for displaying the right-hand strip of a block to form the right side of the box in line 180. The VDU statement of line 190 takes the cursor down one screen line, restates the colour code and displays an 'L' shape for the corner. Line 200 displays the lower side and line 210 displays the bottom right corner.

Calling program: The program begins by putting the computer into Mode 7, for this is the mode in which the procedure is designed to work. The title must consist only of upper-case letters, since the colour codes used make lower-case letters appear as graphics shapes. Use the following colour codes:

red	145
green	146
yellow	147

blue	148
magenta	149
cyan	150
white	151

The X coordinate, which varies according to the length of the title, may be any value from 0 to about 30, or slightly more if the title is short. The Y coordinate may have any value from 0 to 22 (remember that the title and box occupy 3 screen lines). As soon as the details have been entered at lines 20 to 50, the procedure is called and the boxed title is displayed.

Line 70 causes a blank line to be displayed to prevent the usual '>' prompt character from being displayed to the left of the box. Because of the colour codes, it is displayed as a curious shape which spoils the box.

PROCcentral

What it does: Displays a title, centred, on any line.

Formal parameters: Y, the number of the screen line on which the title is to be displayed.
$T\$$, the title.

Local variables: L, the length of $T\$$.
X, the X coordinate of the left-hand end of the title.
C, the number of characters in a screen line in the current mode.

Actual parameters: *taby, title$*.

Listing:

```
10 CLS
20 INPUT "How many lines down? "taby
30 INPUT "TITLE "title$
40 PROCcentral(taby,title$)
50 END
60 REM ************************
70 DEF PROCcentral(Y,T$)
80 LOCAL L,X,C
```

```
 90  C=(?&352+256*?&353)/?&34F
100  L=LEN(T$)
110  X=(C-L)/2
120  PRINT TAB(X,Y)T$
130  ENDPROC
```

How it works: The number of characters in a line (*C*) is calculated in line 90 by using values read from memory. The number of bytes required to store a screen line in the current mode is divided by the number of bytes needed to define a character. This gives the number of characters in a line. *X* is calculated in line 110 by reducing *C* by the number of characters in the title and dividing the result by two. Line 120 displays the title, using the calculated value of *X* and the specified value of *Y*.

Calling program: After stating how many lines down the screen the title is to appear, you are asked to enter the title. PROCcentral then displays the title where required. Note that this procedure can be used in any mode.

Variations: If you intend to use this procedure on a dual processor system, substitute this line for line 90:

   90   C = FNvdudeek (&52)/FNvdupeek (&4F)

Include FNvdudeek and FNvdupeek in the calling program.

PROCcircle

What it does: Draws circles and circular patterns of several kinds.

Formal parameters: $X\%$, X coordinate of the centre of the circle, in graphics units.
   $Y\%$, Y coordinate of the centre of the circle, in graphics units.
   R, radius of the circle initially, in graphics units.
   $T\%$, the type of circle required (see below).
   $P\%$, the kind of periphery (rim) required (see below).
   $C\%$, the colour.

Local variables: $J\%$, the loop index.
   A, the X coordinate of the current point on the periphery, relative to the X coordinate of the centre.

B, the Y coordinate of the current point on the periphery, relative to the Y coordinate of the centre.

C, the value of *B* for the previous point.

D, a constant equal to COS(2*PI/100).

E, a constant equal to SIN(2*PI/100).

Actual parameters: *tabx%*, *taby%*, *radius*, *type%*, *periphery%*, *colour%*.

Listing:

```
 10 MODE 1
 20 INPUT "X,Y,radius,type,periphery,c
olour-"tabx%,taby%,radius,type%,peripher
y%,colour%
 30 PROCcircle(tabx%,taby%,radius,type
%,periphery%,colour%)
 40 END
 50 REM ***************************
 60 DEF PROCcircle(X%,Y%,R,T%,P%,C%)
 70 LOCAL J%,A,B,C,D,E
 80 D=0.9980267283E=6.27905195E-2
 90 GCOL 0,C%
100 MOVE X%+R,Y%+C
110 FOR J%=1 TO 100
120     A=R*D-C*E
130     B=R*E+C*D
140     PLOT P%,X%+A,Y%+B
150     PLOT T%,X%,Y%
160     MOVE X%+A,Y%+B
170     R=A:C=B
180     NEXT
190 ENDPROC
```

How it works: Line 80 assigns values of frequently used constants to variables *D* and *E* to speed the execution of the loop. Line 90 sets the colour of the circle. Line 100 moves the graphics cursor to the centre of the circle.

The remainder of the procedure consists of a loop repeated 100 times to obtain a complete circle. At each repetition, it calculates the coordinates (relative to the centre) of a point on the periphery of the circle (lines 120 and 130). During the first passage through the loop, *R* is the radius and *C* equals zero. *A* is almost equal to *R*, and *B* is very close to zero. Thus the first point is located *R* graphics units to the right of the centre. Leaving out the plotting of the circle for the moment, consider what happens at line 170. The current values of *A* and *B* are assigned to *R* and *C*, respectively. Thus at the next repetition of the loop, these are used as the basis for calculating the next values of *A* and *B*. The equations and constants used in lines 120 and 130 are such that they calculate the position of the current point on the periphery based on the position of the previous point. The loop steps around the periphery in 100 equal steps, so completing a full circle.

At the beginning of each step, the graphics cursor is at a point on the periphery of the circle, where it was left at the end of the previous step. Line 140 moves it along the periphery to the current point just calculated. The PLOT command used here causes a line to be drawn between these two points. It is a straight line, but is a very close approximation to an arc of the circle. By choosing a suitable value for *P%*, the periphery can be plotted as a continuous line, a dotted line, or not plotted at all (giving a pattern without a circular rim).

Line 150 then takes the cursor to the centre of the circle. This draws a line from the periphery to the centre. We shall refer to this as a 'spoke'. By choosing a suitable value for *T%*, the spoke can be plotted as a continuous line, a dotted line, or not plotted at all (giving a plain circle). If *T%* has the value 85 a solid triangular area is plotted, defined by the last three points visited by the cursor. These three points are the previous point on the periphery, the centre of the circle, and the current point on the periphery. This triangle constitutes a sector of the circle (as nearly as makes no difference) so that a solid circle is gradually built up. This completes the plotting and line 160 simply moves the cursor back to the current point on the periphery, ready for the next repetition of the loop.

Calling program: Mode 1 is used in this demonstration, but the procedure works in any of the graphics modes. You are asked to input the parameters as a list, using commas to separate the items. Key in values as follows:

X	Any value in the range 0 to 1279 (try 600 to start with).
Y	Any value in the range 0 to 1023 (try 500).
radius	Any value greater than 0 (try 300).
type	Any one of these four values:

                                              4 gives a plain pattern (no spokes);
                                              5 gives a spoked pattern;
                                              21 gives a dotted spoked pattern;
                                              85 gives a solid circle.

periphery	Any one of these three values:
	4 gives a rimless pattern;
	5 gives a pattern with a rim (i.e. a circle);
	21 gives a pattern with a dotted rim (dotted circle).

colour	Modes 0 and 4	1 (white).
	Modes 1 and 5	1 to 3.
	Mode 2	1 to 15.

Colour zero in any mode gives a pattern in background colour, which is invisible. Another way of getting an invisible pattern is to key 4 for type and 4 for periphery, which gives a pattern with no spokes and no rim – i.e. nothing!

As soon as you have finished keying in all the parameters at line 20 of the calling program, PROCcircle is called to draw the pattern.

The effects of this procedure can be extremely decorative. One effective way of using it is to set up a loop to call the procedure repeatedly, using random numbers for several of the parameters. The screen soon becomes covered with a variety of striking patterns in different colours.

PROCclearscreen

What it does: Clears the screen, starting at the line the cursor is on and finishing at the bottom of the screen.

Formal parameters: None.

Local variables: X, the number of characters per screen line in the current mode.

Y, the number of screen lines in the current mode, minus two.

V, the number of the screen line that the cursor is on when the procedure is called.

J, the loop counter.

Actual parameters: None.

Listing:

```
 10 VDU 31,0,3
 20 INPUT "TEXT "text$
 30 PROCclearscreen
 40 END
 50 REM ***************************
 60 DEF PROCclearscreen
 70 LOCAL X,Y,V,J
 80 X=(?&352+256*?&353)/?&34F
 90 Y=INT(?&354*256/(?&352+256*?&353))
    -2
100 V=VPOS
110 VDU 31,0,V-1
120 FOR J=V TO Y
130    PRINT STRING$(X," ");
140    NEXT
150 PRINT STRING$(X-1," ")
160 VDU 31,0,V-1
170 ENDPROC
```

How it works: The procedure reads certain values from memory to find the value of X (see description of PROCblankline). In line 90, it reads memory to find the number of bytes required for storing the whole screen display, and the number of bytes required for storing a single screen line. Dividing one by the other gives the number of lines in the screen. This value is reduced by 2 to give Y. The VPOS function is used in line 100 to find the line that the cursor is on. Line 110 uses a VDU 31 statement to move the cursor to the beginning of the line above this. This is because it is assumed that the user will have pressed RETURN before the procedure is called, so that the cursor will actually be in the line below that from which clearing is to begin (see Variations below). The loop at lines 120 to 140 prints a series of spaces the full width of the screen, on all lines down to the last but one. Program line 150 then clears the bottom line in the same way, except for the character space at the bottom right corner. The reason for not clearing this space is that this would cause the display to scroll up one line, so losing text displayed on the top line. Finally, program line 160 returns the cursor to the beginning of the line it was on when the clearing began.

Calling program: The most convincing way to demonstrate the procedure is to list the program before running it. This covers most of the screen with the listing, providing plenty of material for the procedure to clear. Then run the program. Line 10 takes the cursor to the fourth screen line before asking for INPUT. If you have listed the program immediately before running it, you will find the INPUT message displayed near the top of the listing. Key in a few words of text, then press RETURN. The procedure clears the screen from the fourth line to the bottom. The fact that the top three lines (above the line the cursor was on) are not cleared, shows that this is not just the ordinary 'CLS' action.

Variations: If you are *not* using RETURN or a PRINT statement with an automatic carriage return immediately before this procedure is called, delete the '−1' from lines 110 and 160. Amend line 120 to 'FOR J=V TO Y−1'.

If you intend to use this program on a dual-processor system, substitute these lines for lines 80 and 90:

```
80   X = FNvdudeek (&52)/FNvdupeek (&4F)
90   Y = INT (FNvdupeek (&54)*256/FNvdudeek(&52))−2
```

Include FNvdupeek and FNvdudeek in the calling program.

PROCdelay

What it does: Makes the computer wait for a specified time before continuing with the program.

Formal parameters: *S*, the delay period, in seconds.

Local variables: *T*, the value of the pseudo-variable *TIME* when the procedure is called.

Actual parameters: *seconds*.

Listing:

```
10 CLS
20 INPUT "Required time in seconds is
"seconds
30 PROCdelay(seconds)
40 PRINT "Time up"
50 END
60 REM ***************************
70 DEF PROCdelay(S)
```

```
 80 LOCAL T
 90 T=TIME:REPEAT UNTIL TIME>T+S*100
100 ENDPROC
```

How it works: As soon as the procedure begins, *T* takes the value of *TIME*. Then follows a loop which is repeated until *TIME* has increased by one hundred times the value of *S*. Since *TIME* is incremented once every hundredth of a second, the loop is repeated for *S* seconds. Then the procedure ends and the program continues.

Calling program: Key in any delay time, in seconds, when asked. There will be a delay for that period, at the end of which the message 'Time up' is displayed. Note that this procedure uses *TIME*, but does not re-set it. Thus it does not interfere with the use of *TIME* in any other part of the program or in any other procedures.

Associated routines: PROCwait.

PROCdelete

What it does: Deletes a word from an alphabetically linked list.

Formal parameters: *D%*, the word (or phrase) to be deleted.

Local variables: *C%*, the number of the word currently being accessed.

Actual parameters: *delete$*.

Global variables: *PC%*, the number of the word accessed previously to word *C%*.
   QC%, the number of the word accessed previously to word *PC%*.
   head%, the pointer to the first word (alphabetically) on the list.

Global arrays: *list$*, the list of words.
   key%, the pointers to the linked list.

Listing:

```
10 DIM list$(10),key%(10)
20 head%=1:key%(1)=0:PC%=1
```

```
   30 CLS
   40 FOR number%=1 TO 10
   50    PRINT "Entry no: ";number%;:INPU
T " "list$(number%)
   60    PROCinsert(number%)
   70    NEXT
   80 CLS
   90 PRINT "Alphabetic list is:"
  100 PROCdisplay
  110 REPEAT:INPUT'"Type item for deleti
on "delete$
  120    PROCdelete(delete$)
  130    PRINT "Amended list is:"
  140    PROCdisplay
  150    UNTIL head%=0:END
  160 DEF PROCinsert(N%)
  170 IF N%=1 THEN 270
  180 LOCAL C%,D$
  190 C%=head%
  200 D$=list$(C%):QC%=PC%:PC%=C%:C%=key
%(C%)
  210 IF C%=0 AND list$(N%)>D$ THEN key%
(N%)=0:key%(PC%)=N%:ENDPROC
  220 IF list$(N%)>D$ THEN 200
  230 IF list$(N%)=D$ THEN ENDPROC
  240 IF PC%=head% THEN head%=N%:key%(N%
)=PC%:ENDPROC
  250 key%(QC%)=N%
  260 key%(N%)=PC%
  270 ENDPROC
  280 DEFPROCdisplay
  290 IF head%=0 THEN PRINT'"List empty"
:
  300 LOCAL C%
  310 C%=head%
  320 PRINT list$(C%)
  330 C%=key%(C%):IF C%>0 THEN 320
  340 ENDPROC
  350 REM ************************
  360 DEF PROCdelete(D$)
  370 IF head%=0 THEN PRINT'"List empty"
:
  380 LOCAL C%
  390 C%=head%
  400 IF list$(C%)<>D$ AND C%>0 THEN REP
```

```
EAT:QC%=PC%:PC%=C%:C%=key%(C%):UNTIL lis
t$(C%)=D$ OR C%=0
  410 IF C%=0 THEN ENDPROC
  420 QC%=PC%:PC%=C%:C%=key%(C%)
  430 IF PC%=head% THEN head%=C%:ENDPROC
  440 key%(QC%)=key%(PC%):PC%=QC%
  450 ENDPROC
```

How it works: For a description of how a linked list is constructed, and of the advantages of using linked lists, see the description of PROCinsert.

Line 370 detects if *head%* has the value zero which indicates that the list contains no entries. If so, a message is displayed and the procedure ends. Otherwise, *C%* takes the value of *head%* (line 390) and the computer begins to work its way through the list. Each word is tested as it is reached (line 400), to see if it is the word to be deleted. If it is not, and the end of the list has not been reached, *C%* takes the value from *key%*() which points to the next word on the list. This process continues until the word to be deleted is found or *C%* acquires the value zero. If the latter occurs, the end of the list has been reached, and the procedure ends (line 410). If the word is found, then line 420 points *C%* to the next word on the list. If *C%* had previously been pointing to the head of the list (i.e. the first word to be deleted), then (at line 430) *head%* is made to point at the next word (previously second on the list), and the procedure ends. If the deleted word is further down the list, line 440 alters the pointer, which previously pointed to the word, to point to the word after it. This ensures that the deleted word is 'missed out' when the list is searched by PROCdisplay or when new words are to be added by PROCinsert. Note that the word is still present in *list$*() even though it can no longer be accessed.

Calling program: This must have lines such as lines 10 and 20 to dimension the global arrays and to initialise the values of certain variables.

After the initialising lines, the calling program asks you to key in ten words. This number is set for convenience in demonstrating the routine. In your own programs it is possible to have any number of words in the list, limited only by the amount of memory required for *list$*() and *key%*().

In addition to single words, you may also enter phrases. As each word is keyed in, it is inserted in the alphabetical list by PROCinsert. When all ten words have been entered, the screen clears and

PROCdisplay is called to display the list. You are then asked to key in the word that is to be deleted (line 110). PROCdelete is called to delete the word, after which PROCdisplay is called again to display the amended list. The deletion routine is repeated, so that you can, if you wish, delete all the words from the list and obtain the 'List empty' message.

Associated routines: PROCinsert, PROCdisplay, PROCdisplayinitial.

PROCdisplay

What it does: Displays a linked list of words in alphabetical order.

Formal parameters: None.

Local variables: *C%*, the number of the word currently being accessed.

Actual parameters: None.

Global variables: *head%*, the pointer to the first word (alphabetically) on the list.

Global arrays: *list$*, the list of words.
    key%, the pointers to the linked list.

Listing:

```
 10  DIM list$(10),key%(10)
 20  head%=1:key%(1)=0:PC%=1
 30  CLS
 40  FOR number%=1 TO 10
 50    PRINT "Entry no: ";number%;:INPU
T " "list$(number%)
 60    PROCinsert(number%)
 70    NEXT
 80  CLS
 90  PRINT "Alphabetic list is:"
100  PROCdisplay
110  END
120  REM ************************
```

```
130 DEF PROCinsert(N%)
140 IF N%=1 THEN ENDPROC
150 LOCAL C%,D$
160 C%=head%
170 D$=list$(C%):QC%=PC%:PC%=C%:C%=key
%(C%)
180 IF C%=0 AND list$(N%)>D$ THEN key%
(N%)=0:key%(PC%)=N%:ENDPROC
190 IF list$(N%)>D$ THEN 170
200 IF list$(N%)=D$ THEN ENDPROC
210 IF PC%=head% THEN head%=N%:key%(N%
)=PC%:ENDPROC
220 key%(QC%)=N%
230 key%(N%)=PC%
240 ENDPROC
250 REM ***************************
260 DEFPROCdisplay
270 IF head%=0 THEN PRINT'"List empty"
:ENDPROC
280 LOCAL C%
290 C%=head%
300 PRINT list$(C%)
310 C%=key%(C%):IF C%>0 THEN 300
320 ENDPROC
```

How it works: For a description of how a linked list is constructed, and of the advantages of using linked lists, see the description of PROCinsert.

Line 270 detects if *head%* has the value zero which indicates that the list contains no entries. If so, a message is displayed and the procedure ends. Otherwise, *C%* takes the value of *head%* (line 290) and the computer begins to work its way through the list. Each word is displayed as it is reached (line 300). Then *C%* takes the value from *key%* ()which points to the next word on the list. This process continues until *C%* acquires the value zero. This indicates that the end of the list has been reached and the procedure ends.

Calling program: This must have lines such as lines 10 and 20 to dimension the global arrays and to initialise the values of certain variables.

After the initialising lines, the calling program asks you to key in ten words. This number is set for convenience in demonstrating the routine. In your own programs it is possible to have any number of

words in the list, limited only by the amount of memory required for
list.$() and *key%()*. In addition to single words, you may also enter
phrases. As each word is keyed in, it is inserted in the alphabetical list by
PROCinsert. When all ten words have been entered, the screen clears
and PROCdisplay is called to display the list in alphabetical order.

Associated routines: PROCinsert, PROCdisplayinitial, PROCdelete.

PROCdisplayinitial

What it does: Displays words beginning with a specified letter or
sequence of letters, taken from a linked list.

Formal parameters: *I$*, the initial letter or sequence of letters.

Local variables: *C%*, the number of the word currently being accessed.
L%, the length of I$.

Actual parameters: *initial$*.

Global variables: *head%*, the pointer to the first word (alphabetically)
on the list.

Global arrays: *list$*, the list of words.
key%, the pointers to the linked list.

Listing:

```
10 DIM list$(10),key%(10)
20 head%=1:key%(1)=0:PC%=1
30 CLS
40 FOR number%=1 TO 10
50    PRINT "Entry no: ";number%;:INPU
T" "list$(number%)
60    PROCinsert(number%)
70    NEXT
80 INPUT "Type initial letter(s)"init
ial$
90 CLS
100 PRINT "Items beginning with '"init
ial$"' are:"
```

```
110 PROCdisplayinitial(initial$)
120 END
130 DEF PROCinsert(N%)
140 IF N%=1 THEN ENDPROC
150 LOCAL C%,D$
160 L%=0:C%=head%
170 D$=list$(C%):QC%=PC%:PC%=C%:C%=key
%(C%)
180 IF C%=0 AND list$(N%)>D$ THEN key%
(N%)=0:key%(PC%)=N%:ENDPROC
190 IF list$(N%)>D$ THEN 170
200 IF list$(N%)=D$ THEN ENDPROC
210 IF PC%=head% THEN head%=N%:key%(N%
)=PC%:ENDPROC
220 key%(QC%)=N%
230 key%(N%)=PC%
240 ENDPROC
250 REM ************************
260 DEFPROCdisplayinitial(I$)
270 IF head%=0 THEN PRINT'"List empty"
:ENDPROC
280 LOCAL C%,L%
290 C%=head%:L%=LEN(I$)
300 IF LEFT$(list$(C%),L%)=I$ THEN PRI
NT list$(C%)
310 C%=key%(C%):IF C%>0 THEN 300
320 ENDPROC
```

How it works: For a description of how a linked list is constructed, and of the advantages of using linked lists, see the description of PROCinsert.

Line 270 detects if *head%* has the value zero which indicates that the list contains no entries. If so, a message is displayed and the procedure ends. Otherwise, *C%* takes the value of *head%* (line 290) and the computer begins to work its way through the list. Each word is tested as it is reached (line 300), to see if it begins with *I$*. If so, it is displayed. Then *C%* takes the value from *key%()* which points to the next word on the list. This process continues until *C%* acquires the value zero. This indicates that the end of the list has been reached and the procedure ends.

Calling program: This must have lines such as lines 10 and 20 to dimension the global arrays and to initialise the values of certain variables.

After the initialising lines, the calling program asks you to key in ten words. This number is set for convenience in demonstrating the routine. In your own programs it is possible to have any number of words in the list, limited only by the amount of memory required for *list*$() and *key*%(). In addition to single words, you may also enter phrases. As each word is keyed in, it is inserted in the alphabetical list by PROCinsert. When all ten words have been entered, you are asked to key in the letter or letters for which a search is to be made. The screen clears and PROCdisplayinitial is called to display words from the list beginning with the letter or letters, in alphabetical order.

Associated routines: PROCinsert, PROCdisplay, PROCdelete.

PROCdoke

What it does: Stores a value (0-65536) in two consecutive bytes of memory.

Formal parameters: V, the value.
A, the first of the two memory addresses.

Local variables: None.

Actual parameters: *value, address*$.

Listing:

```
 10 MODE 4
 20 INPUT "Value (0-65535) "value
 30 INPUT "Base address (HEX) "address
    $
 40 address=EVAL("&"+address$)
 50 PROCdoke(value,address)
 60 END
 70 REM ************************
 80 DEF PROCdoke(V,A)
 90 ?A=V MOD 256
100 A?1=V DIV 256
110 ENDPROC
```

How it works: The MOD operator gives the integer value of the remainder when the value *V* is divided by 256. This is stored in the first of the two addresses (*A*). This is often referred to as the low byte. Then the DIV operator gives the integer result (the quotient) of dividing *V* by 256. This is stored in the next address after *A*. It is referred to as the high byte.

Calling program: The program first asks you to type in the value to be stored, then the base address (i.e. the address at which the byte is to be stored). Type in the value in decimal but type in the address in hexadecimal (but not preceded by "&"). Line 40 adds the "&" to *address*$ and then evaluates it as a hexadecimal number. Which is used as an actual parameter. The function will then store the number. If you enter an address such as &7000 (key only '7000'), which is an address in video RAM near the centre of the screen, you will see irregular marks appear on the screen. This indicates that the value has been stored.

Associated functions: FNdeek.

PROCdoubleheight

What it does: Produces double-height text in Mode 7.

Formal parameters: *X*, *Y*, the TAB position at which the text is to be displayed.
   B, code for background colour.
   F, code for foreground colour.
   FL, code for flashing or not.
   M$, the message to be displayed.

Local variables: *J*, the loop index.

Actual parameters: *tabx*, *taby*, *background*, *foreground*, *flashing*, *message*$.

Listing:

```
 10 MODE 7
 20 INPUT "MESSAGE "message$
 30 INPUT "ENTER THE X COORDINATE "tab
x
 40 INPUT "ENTER THE Y COORDINATE "tab
y
 50 INPUT "SELECT BACKGROUND COLOUR "b
ackground
 60 INPUT "SELECT FOREGROUND COLOUR "f
oreground
 70 INPUT "FLASHING? "flashing
 80 PROCdoubleheight(tabx,taby,backgro
und,foreground,flashing,message$)
 90 PRINT
100 END
110 REM ***************************
120 DEF PROCdoubleheight(X,Y,B,F,FL,M$
)
130 LOCAL J
140 FOR J=0 TO 1
150    PRINT TAB(X,Y+J);:VDU 141,B,157,
F,FL
160    PRINT M$;"   ";:VDU 156
170    NEXT
180 ENDPROC
```

How it works: Double-height text is displayed by first printing the code 141, then displaying the same text on two consecutive lines of the screen. On the upper of the two lines only the top half of each character is displayed. On the line below only the lower half of each character is displayed. These lines combine to give double-height text.

The text is displayed twice by the loop (lines 140 to 170), in which *J* first equals zero, then equals 1. The text is first displayed at TAB(X,Y) and then at TAB(X,Y+1), i.e. at the same horizontal position on the line below.

The VDU 141 statement of line 150 turns on double-height mode. This is followed by the code for the colour of the background. The code 157 indicates that the previous code is to be used to define background colour. Then comes the code for foreground colour, (*F*), and the code which determines whether or not the foreground colour is to flash. (*FL*). Line 160 displays the message, top half on the first time through the loop, bottom half on the second time through. The three spaces after the message compensate for the character positions occupied by the control codes to the left of the message. The VDU 156 statement restores the background colour to black.

Calling program: The program starts by putting the computer into Mode 7. Then lines 20 to 70 ask for the message and the various parameters required. The message may have up to 32 characters. The X coordinate may have any value from 0 up to about 30 (allowing for the length of the message). The Y coordinate may range from 0 to 24. The background and foreground colour codes range from 129 to 135. For flashing text use code 136; for non-flashing text, use 137. The procedure is then called and the double-height message is displayed.

PROCexplode

What it does: Produces a visual display and the sound of an explosion at any specified position.

Formal parameters: *X, Y,* the graphics coordinates of the centre of the explosion.

Local variables: *J,* the loop index.

Actual parameters: *tabx, taby.*

Listing:

```
 10 MODE 2
 20 INPUT "Enter the X coordinate, 50
to 1229 "tabx
 30 INPUT "Enter the Y coordinate, 50
to 973 "taby
 40 PROCexplode(tabx,taby)
 50 END
 60 REM ***************************
 70 DEF PROCexplode(X,Y)
 80 LOCAL J
 90 VDU 23,224,152,10,97,8,80,38,10,16
1
100 VDU 5
110 FOR J=1 TO 45
120    SOUND 0,INT(J/3)-15,6,2
```

```
130    GCOL  0,RND(16)-1
140    MOVE  X-50+RND(100),Y-50+RND(100)
:VDU 224
150    NEXT
160 VDU 4
170 ENDPROC
```

How it works: Line 90 defines character 224 as an irregular pattern of dots. The VDU 5 statement of line 100 causes this pattern to be displayed (later, in line 140) at the position of the graphics cursor.

The loop of lines 110 to 150 displays the cloud of dots 45 times. An explosive noise is generated at line 120. As *J* increases, the amplitude is increased from -15 to 0, so reducing the volume of the sound from its maximum to silence. This makes the sound of the explosion die away gradually. Line 130 chooses a graphics colour at random, having any value between 0 and 15. All the Mode 2 colours, including the flashing ones, are likely to appear in the display. Line 140 moves the graphics cursor to a random position within 50 graphics units from left to right and from top to bottom of the central position of the explosion. As the cursor is moved, the VDU 224 statement of line 140 causes the pattern of dots to be displayed at the cursor position. The effect of this is to make a large, diffuse, multicoloured cloud. The cloud remains on the screen after the procedure is finished.

Calling program: You key in the required X and Y screen positions, within the limits stated. The procedure is then called and the explosion occurs.

PROCgunfire

What it does: Produces the sound of gunfire (single shot).

Formal parameters: None.

Local variables: None.

Actual parameters: None.

Listing:

```
 10 PROCgunfire
 20 END
 30 REM ************************
 40 DEF PROCgunfire
 50 ENVELOPE 1,1,0,0,0,0,0,0,126,-2,0,
-4,126,126
 60 SOUND 0,1,6,8
 70 ENDPROC
```

How it works: Line 50 defines ENVELOPE 1 with the shortest possible step length, (1), and no change in pitch, (0,0,0,0,0,0). Attack is at maximum rate, (126), giving an explosive sound that begins at maximum amplitude. Amplitude falls very slightly during the decay phase, (−2), and not at all, (0), in the sustain phase, keeping the sound at almost maximum volume. It falls slightly (−4) during the release phase, so obtaining a 'short, sharp' explosive effect. Target levels are set high (126,126) to maintain maximum volume.

The SOUND statement at line 60 uses the noise channel (channel 0) and ENVELOPE 1 (just defined). The 'pitch' is a low-frequency white noise, (6), and the duration is 0.4 seconds, (8).

Calling program: When the program is run, the procedure is called and the sound is heard. In your own programs it is a good idea to reserve ENVELOPE 1 for this procedure and for any other sound effects procedures that may be used. Then, ENVELOPE 1 is redefined each time one of these procedures is called. The other envelopes may then be defined globally at the beginning of the program to provide for musical tones and tunes.

Variations: To produce the sounds of different kinds of gun, try altering the pitch of the SOUND command; change the 6 in line 60 to 4 or 5.

PROCinsert

What it does: Builds up a linked list of words that can be accessed in alphabetical order.

Formal parameters: $N\%$, the number of the word in the list, in order of entry.

Local variables: *C%*, the number of the word currently being accessed. *D$*, the word currently being compared with other words in the list.

Actual parameters: *number%*.

Global variables: *PC%*, the number of the word accessed previously to word *C%*.

QC%, the number of the word accessed previously to word *PC%*.
head%, the pointer to the first word (alphabetically) on the list.

Global arrays: *list$*, the list of words.
key%, the pointers to the linked list.

Listing:

```
   10 DIM list$(10),key%(10)
   20 head%=1:key%(1)=0:PC%=1
   30 CLS
   40 FOR number%=1 TO 10
   50    PRINT "Entry no: ";number%;:INPU
T" "list$(number%)
   60    PROCinsert(number%)
   70    NEXT
   80 CLS
   90 PRINT "Alphabetic list is:"
  100 PROCdisplay
  110 END
  120 REM ***************************
  130 DEF PROCinsert(N%)
  140 IF N%=1 THEN ENDPROC
  150 LOCAL C%,D$
  160 C%=head%
  170 D$=list$(C%):QC%=PC%:PC%=C%:C%=key
%(C%)
  180 IF C%=0 AND list$(N%)>D$ THEN key%
(N%)=0:key%(PC%)=N%:ENDPROC
  190 IF list$(N%)>D$ THEN 170
  200 IF list$(N%)=D$ THEN ENDPROC
  210 IF PC%=head% THEN head%=N%:key%(N%
)=PC%:ENDPROC
  220 key%(QC%)=N%
  230 key%(N%)=PC%
  240 ENDPROC
  250 REM ***************************
```

```
260 DEFPROCdisplay
270 IF head%=0 THEN PRINT'"List empty"
:ENDPROC
280 LOCAL C%
290 C%=head%
300 PRINT list$(C%)
310 C%=key%(C%):IF C%>0 THEN 300
320 ENDPROC
```

How it works: The procedure establishes a linked list of words, arranged in alphabetical order. The words are held in *list*$(), in the order in which they are typed in (or otherwise added to the list), which is not necessarily in alphabetical order. The variable *head%* and the entries in the array *key%*() are such as to make the computer read the words in alphabetical order. To begin with, *head%* points to the head of the list, i.e. the location in *list*$() which contains the first word alphabetically. For example, if the first word was 'ATOM' and was stored at *list*$(6), then *head%* would have the value 6. The pointer to the next word on the list is stored at the corresponding location in *key%*(). In the example above, *key%*(6) would hold this pointer. If the second word on the list was 'BEEB', stored in *list*$(3), the value in *key%*(6), would be 3. The values in *key%*() point the way from one location in *word*$() to the next. The last word in the list has 0 in the corresponding location of *key%*(). So, when the pointer is 0, it is known that the end of the list has been reached.

The values of *head%*, *key%* and *PC%* are set (at line 20 of the calling program) before the procedure is called for the first time. They are set ready to point to the first entry in the list, which will be stored at *list*$(1). Thus, at line 140, the procedure does nothing further when the first entry is made. When the second and subsequent entries are made, the computer searches the list, in alphabetical order, to find the point at which the new entry is to be inserted. It uses *C%* to access each entry in turn. *C%* is first given the value of *head%* to take the computer to the head of the list. At each stage after this *C%* takes its value from *key%*(), as explained above. Each time the computer accesses a new location (line 170), the values previously held in *C%* are passed to *PC%* and then to *QC%* so that the computer 'remembers where it has been' for the previous two stages. Line 180 deals with the occasion on which the newly entered word comes last in the alphabetical list. Its key is made zero (i.e. the new end of list) and the key of the previously accessed word, (the one that used to be the last), is now made to point to the new last word.

Line 190 sends the computer back to line 170 to access the next word if the end of the list has not been reached and the word currently being accessed comes before the new entry. If the accessed word is the same as the new entry, or should come after it alphabetically, the correct place for insertion has been found. The program moves on to line 200 which ends the procedure if the newly entered word is already in the list. Line 210 deals with inserting a word which is to be at the head of the list; it alters *head%* to point to the new word, and the pointer in *key%()* to point to the previous head of list. Otherwise the new word is inserted between two existing words by lines 220 and 230. Line 220 alters the pointer, which previously pointed to the word after the new word, making it point to the new word. Line 230 sets the pointer corresponding to the new word to point to the word after the new word.

A linked list is ideal for building indexes, catalogues and other kinds of lists that need adding to a word, (or a group of words), at a time. It is particularly useful in the BBC Micro since the words are never moved around in *list.$()* after they have first been entered. Inserting a new word in the list is done by storing it in the next vacant location in list.$(), and then adjusting the pointers in *head%* or *key%()* accordingly. Moving strings around in memory is particularly wasteful of memory in the BBC machine, but if the strings are not moved and only the numeric pointers are altered, no memory is wasted. In addition, altering values in arrays is faster than moving strings in arrays.

Calling program: This must have lines such as lines 10 and 20 to dimension the global arrays and to initialise the values of certain variables. It should be noted that this procedure has global variables. We need these to carry various values between the calling program and the procedure and between the procedure and the related procedures. This is an example of a program in which it is necessary to use global variables. One of the related procedures, PROCdisplay appears at the end of the program. It is needed to display the content of the list in alphabetical order.

After the initialising lines, the calling program asks you to key in ten words. The number is set for convenience in demonstrating the routine. In your own programs it is possible to have any number of words in the list, limited only by the amount of memory required for *list.$()* and *key%()*. In addition to single words, you may also enter phrases. As each word is keyed in, it is inserted in the alphabetical list by PROCinsert. When all ten words have been entered, the screen clears and PROCdisplay is called to display the list in alphabetical order.

Associated routines: PROCdisplay, PROCdisplayinitial, PROC-delete.

PROCinvisible

What it does: Allows a display to be built up invisibly and then made visible instantaneously.

Formal parameters: *C*, the screen colour while the display is being built.

Local variables: *J*, the loop index.

Actual parameters: *colour*.

Listing:

```
 10 MODE 4
 20 INPUT "Select a colour 0 to 15 - "
colour
 30 PROCinvisible(colour)
 40 PRINT "This was invisible"
 50 T=TIME:REPEAT UNTIL TIME>T+500
 60 VDU 20
 70 END
 80 REM ************************
 90 DEF PROCinvisible(C)
100 LOCAL J
110 FOR J=0 TO 15
120   VDU 19,J,C,0;0;0;
130   NEXT J
140 ENDPROC
```

How it works: The procedure works in all graphics modes. The procedure consists of a loop which defines all the logical colours (from 0 to 15) to the actual colour, *C*. The effect of this is that a display may now be built up using all the logical colours allowed in the current mode. Although these colours are logically different, they are all made the same actual colour by the procedure. Apart from the cursor, the screen is a blank expanse of colour *C*.

Calling program: You are asked to select any colour – not restricted to the default range normally available in the current mode. As soon as you have done this, the procedure is called and the whole screen changes to the colour you have selected. Only the cursor is visible. Line 40 PRINTs a message, but, because logical background colours and logical foreground colours have now been made the same actual colour, the message is invisible. You could add other lines to the calling program between lines 40 and 50 to build up an even more complex display. The delay loop at line 50 is just to give you time to see the blank screen. Then line 60 uses the VDU 20 statement. The effect of this is to restore all logical colours to their default values. As a result, the message and the text displayed earlier become visible instantaneously.

Complicated graphics displays take an appreciable time to build up on the screen. It gives a program greater polish if this procedure is called and the display is built up invisibly. When all is ready, a single VDU 20 statement reveals the completed display.

PROCkeys

What it does: Controls the state of the SHIFT, SHIFT LOCK and CAPS LOCK keys from the program.

Formal parameters: *C$*, the choice string.

Local variables: None.

Actual parameters: *choice$*.

Listing:

```
10 CLS
20 PRINT "Shift lock on? Type SLO"
30 PRINT "Caps lock on? Type CLO"
40 PRINT "Lower case? Type LC"
50 INPUT "Type choice "choice$
60 PROCkeys(choice$)
70 END
```

```
 80  REM  ************************
 90  DEF  PROCkeys(C$)
100  IF  C$="SLO"  THEN  ?602=&10
110  IF  C$="CLO"  THEN  ?602=&20
120  IF  C$="LC"  THEN  ?602=&30
130  ENDPROC
```

How it works: The key which is to be affected is determined by the value of *C$*. Depending on this value, a value is stored at address 602 in memory. This sets the required keys.

Calling program: Lines 20 to 40 tell you what to key in to control the chosen key. The INPUT statement of line 50 accepts your choice. Watch the red lamps (CAPS LOCK and SHIFT LOCK) to the left of the space bar as you press RETURN. As PROCkeys is called, one or both of the lamps may change state. The program has ended, so try typing a few characters to confirm that the change of state has taken effect.

PROCload

What it does: Loads data from disk or tape and stores it in a block of RAM. The equivalent of the operating system statement *LOAD.

Formal parameters: *F$*, the file name.
   S$, the base (or start) address of the block of memory, in hexadecimal.

Local variables: *B*, the length of the string to be stored in the file string buffer.
   fsbuffer, the base address of the file string buffer.

Actual parameters: *file$*, *start$*.

Listing:

```
10  MODE 7
20  PRINT'
30  INPUT "Enter file name "file$
40  INPUT "Enter start address (hex) "
start$
```

```
 50 PROCload(file$,start$)
 60 REM **************************
 70 END
 80 DEFPROCload(F$,S$)
 90 LOCAL B,fsbuffer
100 B=LEN(F$+S$)+6
110 DIM fsbuffer B+1
120 X%=fsbuffer MOD 256:Y%=fsbuffer DI
V 256
130 $fsbuffer="LOAD "+F$+" "+S$
140 CALL &FFF7
150 ENDPROC
```

How it works: The file string buffer is to be filled with a string which is to be used as a command sent to the command line interpreter routine (CLI). We must first calculate *B*, the length of the string. The string has the format

   LOAD NAME SSSS

in which NAME is the file number under which the data has been saved, and SSSS is the base address of the block of memory into which it is to be loaded. The length of this string is calculated in line 100, with 6 bytes added to allow for the word LOAD and the spaces required in the string. This done, a small block of memory (the file string buffer) is set aside in line 110 to hold the string. The value of *fsbuffer* is the base address of this block. This value is converted into two bytes and assigned to $X\%$ (low byte) and $Y\%$ (high byte) by line 120. The string indirection operator, '$', is used in line 130 to store the concatenated command string in the file string buffer. Line 140 calls the operating system command line interpreter routine (OSCLI). When this is done, the values of $X\%$ and $Y\%$ are automatically loaded into the X and Y registers of the microprocessor, so passing to the CLI routines the address at which the command statement is to be found. This statement is then executed and data is read from disk or tape and stored in the specified block of memory.

Calling program: The calling program puts the computer into Mode 7 for the purposes of the demonstration, though the procedure will work in any mode.

   Before running the calling program, you should have saved a file, using PROCsave. Place the disk in the drive or, if you used a tape, place it in the recorder, rewound to the correct position. Run the program and key in the file name under which the data was saved. Then key in the starting address in hexadecimal, but not preceded by an '&'. This need not be the same address as the address from which the data was saved. For the demonstration, use the value 7C00 which is the base address of screen memory in Mode 7. As soon as you have entered these details, PROCload is called. If you are using disks, the data will be loaded automatically. If you are using tape, the message 'Searching' will be displayed. Press PLAY on the recorder. As the data is loaded, the text which is already on the screen is replaced, character by character, by the text which was on the screen when you used PROCsave.

Associated routines: PROCsave.

PROCmean

What it does: Asks for the values in a sample to be keyed in and calculates their mean.

Formal parameters: *S*, the number of values in the sample.

Local variables: *number*, the value currently keyed in.
total, the cumulative total of the values.
J, the loop index.

Actual parameters: *sample*.

Listing:

```
 10 CLS
 20 INPUT "How many in the sample "sam
ple
 30 PROCmean(sample)
 40 END
 50 REM ***************************
 60 DEF PROCmean(S)
 70 LOCAL number,total,J
 80 PRINT "Enter the numbers"
 90 REPEAT
100   INPUT number
110   J=J+1
120   total=total+number
```

```
130    UNTIL J=S
140 PRINT "The mean is ";total/S
150 ENDPROC
```

How it works: The procedure first displays a message inviting the user to key in the sample values. Then a loop (lines 90 to 130) waits for each number to be input. As each is keyed in, *J*, is incremented (line 110), so counting how many values have been entered. The total of all values entered accumulates as *total*. The loop repeats until *J* attains the same value as *S*. Then the computer drops out of the loop. It divides the total by the number of values to find the mean, displays the mean value, and the procedure ends.

Calling program: You are asked how many values there are to be in the sample. The procedure is called (line 30) and accepts that number of values, after which it displays the mean.

PROCmoveacross

What it does: Moves a block of user-defined graphics characters across the screen.

Formal parameters: *D*, the distance it is to be moved.
   Y, the screen line along which it is to be moved.
   C, the ASCII code for the left-most character of the block.

Local variables: *X*, loop index, the current horizontal TAB position of the left-most character.
   T, timing loop index.

Actual parameters: *distance, taby, code*.

Listing:

```
10 MODE 4
20 INPUT "Enter chosen ASCII code-224
TO 254 "code
30 INPUT "Enter chosen Y coordinate-0
TO 31 "taby
```

```
   40 INPUT "Enter chosen X distance-0 t
o 37 "distance
   50 VDU 23,code,0,126,63,31,7,15,31,36
   60 VDU 23,code+1,0,12,143,208,224,192
,128,0
   70 CLS
   80 PROCmoveacross(distance,taby,code)
   90 END
  100 REM ***********************
  110 DEF PROCmoveacross(D,Y,C)
  120 VDU 23,1,0;0;0;0;
  130 LOCAL X,T
  140 FOR X=0 TO D
  150    PRINT TAB(X,Y)"  "TAB(X+1,Y)CHR$
(C)CHR$(C+1);
  160    FOR T=1 TO 300:NEXT
  170    NEXT
  180 VDU 23,1,1;0;0;0;
  190 ENDPROC
```

How it works: Line 120 disables the cursor, so that it does not spoil the display. The illusion of motion is obtained by displaying the same block of characters in successive positions from left to right across the screen. After a block has been displayed, there is a pause to allow it to be seen. Then it is blanked out by displaying a block of spaces in the same position. The block is then re-displayed, but in a position further to the right. This sequence is repeated, moving the block across the screen.

This operation is performed as a loop (lines 140 to 170) in which the loop index (X) determines the horizontal position of the characters. The procedure is written to move a block of two characters, but it is easy to adapt the routine to move blocks of three, four or even more characters, providing they are for a horizontal block.

The first step is to display a block of two spaces (line 150). There are no characters to be blanked out at this stage, but it is convenient to do the blanking at this stage of the routine. Line 150 continues by displaying the block of characters one TAB position to the right. Line 160 is a loop nested within the main loop to provide the delay. The main loop then repeats, with X incremented by 1. Hence the two spaces now blank out the characters already on the screen and these are re-displayed one TAB position to the right. The loop repeats D times, moving the block across the screen for the required distance. Before the procedure ends, line 180 re-enables the cursor.

Calling program: The program begins by putting the computer into Mode 4, but the procedure may be used (with suitable ranges for the X and Y coordinates) in any mode. The program contains VDU statements at lines 50 and 60 to define two characters which form the image of a bird, flying from left to right. Before these statements are used, you are asked at line 20 to decide which pair of ASCII codes are to be used. Then you are asked to say across which line the bird is to fly, (Y), and for what distance, (X). Depending on the value you key in for X, the bird starts at the left-hand side of the screen and flies that number of TAB positions to the right. Line 80 calls the procedure and the bird flies across the screen.

Variations: Many graphics designs can be used in conjunction with this procedure – other animals, cars, boats, planes and spacecraft can all be made to move across the screen in this way. To make the object begin at a distance from the left-hand side of the screen, alter the 0 in line 140 to a suitable value. To speed up the motion, reduce the 300 in line 160. To make the object move more slowly, increase the 300 to, say, 600. You can have several pairs of characters defined to produce different kinds of birds, cars etc. and, by using different values for 'code' each time you call the procedure in your program, produce a variety of visual effects.
   Finally, to make the object move from right to left, alter line 140 to

   140   FOR X=D TO 1 STEP −1

and alter the X+1 in line 150 to X−1.

Associated routines: PROCmovedown.

PROCmovedown

What it does: Moves a block of user-defined graphics characters down the screen.

Formal parameters: D, the distance the block is to be moved.
   X, the screen column down which it is to be moved.
   C, the ASCII code for the top character of the block.

Local variables: Y, loop index, the current vertical TAB position of the top character.
   J, loop index, for displaying a sequence of characters or spaces.

T, timing loop index.

Actual parameters: *distance, tabx, code.*

Listing:

```
 10 MODE 4
 20 INPUT "Enter chosen ASCII code-224
to 254 "code
 30 INPUT "Enter chosen X coordinate-0
to 39 "tabx
 40 INPUT "Enter chosen Y distance-0 t
o 28 "distance
 50 VDU 23,code,16,16,16,16,16,16,16,1
6
 60 VDU 23,code+1,146,84,56,16,0,0,0,0

 70 CLS
 80 PROCmovedown(distance,tabx,code)
 90 END
100 REM ***************************
110 DEF PROCmovedown(D,X,C)
120 LOCAL Y,J,T
130 VDU 23,1,0;0;0;0;
140 FOR Y=0 TO D
150   FOR J=0 TO 1
160     PRINT TAB(X,Y+J)" "
170     NEXT
180   FOR J=0 TO 1
190     PRINT TAB(X,Y+J+1)CHR$(C+J)
200     NEXT
210   FOR T=1 TO 300:NEXT
220   NEXT
230 VDU 23,1,1;0;0;0;
240 ENDPROC
```

How it works: Line 130 disables the cursor, so that it does not spoil the display. The illusion of motion is obtained by displaying the same block of characters in successive positions from the top to the bottom of the screen. After a block has been displayed, there is a pause to allow it to be seen. Then it is blanked out by displaying a block of spaces in the same position. The block is then re-displayed but in a position further down the screen. This sequence is repeated, moving the block down the screen.

This operation is performed as a loop, (lines 140 to 220), in which the loop index, (*Y*), determines the vertical position of the characters. The procedure is written to move a block of two characters, one above the other, but it is easy to adapt the routine to move a vertical block of three four or more characters.

The first step is to display a block of two spaces, one below the other. The loop in lines 150 to 170 does this. There are no characters to be blanked out at this stage, but it is convenient to do the blanking at this stage of the routine. The next loop, (lines 180 to 200), displays the block of characters, the top one being one line further down the screen than the uppermost of the two spaces just displayed. Line 210 is a loop to provide the delay. The main loop then repeats, with *Y* incremented by 1. Hence the two spaces now blank out the characters already on the screen and the characters are re-displayed one line further down. The loop repeats *D* times, moving the block down the screen for the required distance. Before the procedure ends, line 230 re-enables the cursor.

Calling program: The program begins by putting the computer into Mode 4, but the procedure may be used (with suitable ranges for the X and Y coordinates) in any mode. The program contains VDU statements at lines 50 and 60 to define two characters which form the image of a downward pointing arrow. Before these statements are used, you are asked at line 20 to decide which pair of ASCII codes are to be used. Then you are asked to say down which screen column the arrow is to fall, (X), and for what distance, (Y). Depending on the value you key in for Y, the arrow starts at the top of the screen and falls that number of rows. Line 80 calls the procedure and the arrow falls down the screen.

Variations: There are many graphics designs that can be used in conjunction with this procedure – rockets, aliens from outer space, bombs and raindrops can all be made to move down the screen in this way. To make the object begin at a distance from the top of the screen, alter the 0 in line 140 to a suitable value. To speed up the motion, reduce the 300 in line 210. To make the object move more slowly, increase the 300 to, say, 600. You can have several pairs of characters defined to produce different objects and, by using different values for *code* each time you call the procedure in your program, produce a variety of visual effects.

Finally, to make the object move upwards, from bottom to top, alter line 140 to

140   FOR Y=D TO 1 STEP −1

and alter the Y+J+1 in line 190 to Y+J−1.

Associated routines: PROCmoveacross.

PROCpolygon

What it does: Plots a polygon in any required colour, given the coordinates of its corners.

Formal parameters: *C*, the colour of the polygon.
   N, the number of sides of the polygon.

Local variables: *J*, the loop index.

Actual parameters: *colour, sides.*

Global arrays: *polygon*, the graphics coordinates of the corners of the polygon.

Listing:

```
 10 MODE 4
 20 DIM polygon(15,1)
 30 INPUT "How many sides (3-15) "side
s
 40 PRINT "Key X and Y coordinates"
 50 FOR J=1 TO sides
 60    PRINT "Corner ";J;:INPUT " "poly
gon(J,0),polygon(J,1)
 70    NEXT
 80 INPUT "Select a colour "colour
 90 MODE 2
100 PROCpolygon(colour,sides)
110 END
120 REM *************************
130 DEF PROCpolygon(C,N)
140 LOCAL J
150 MOVEpolygon(1,0),polygon(1,1)
160 GCOL 0,C
```

```
170 FOR J=2 TO N
180    DRAWpolygon(J,0),polygon(J,1)
190    NEXT
200 DRAWpolygon(1,0),polygon(1,1)
210 ENDPROC
```

How it works: The graphics cursor is moved to the position of the first corner of the polygon (line 150). Line 160 sets the foreground colour to that specified for drawing the polygon. Then a loop moves the cursor to each of the other corners in turn, plotting a line of the required colour as it moves (lines 170 to 190). Finally, line 200 draws a line from the last of the corners to the first corner, so completing the polygon.

Calling program: The array dimensioned in line 20 allows for the polygon to have up to 15 sides. You need not alter this for polygons with fewer than 15 sides. If you wish to draw polygons with more than 15 sides, increase the '15' accordingly. You are asked how many sides you require, and then for the X and Y coordinates. Key in the coordinates as pairs of values, each separated by a comma. These coordinates are the ordinary graphics coordinates ranging from 0 to 1279 for X and 0 to 1023 for Y, as explained in Chapter 8 of the User Guide. As you enter each pair of values, the X coordinate is stored in *polygon* (J,0) and the Y coordinate is stored in *polygon* (J,1).

The value that you can enter for colour depends on which mode the computer is in. The calling program puts the computer into Mode 2 (line 90) before calling the procedure, but you can substitute any other graphics mode for this. (Note that the program begins by putting the computer into Mode 4, to make it easier to read the input messages after having been in Mode 2.) The range of values input for the colour should be:

Modes 0 and 4	1
Modes 1 and 5	1–3
Mode 2	1–15

Entering zero in any mode gives an invisible polygon in background colour! This technique can be used (in your own programs) for deleting a polygon which has already been drawn.

Associated routines: PROCsolidpolygon.

PROCquicksortnumber

What it does: Sorts, in ascending order, a set of numeric values in an array.

Formal parameters: *F%*, the first location in the array to be included in the sort.

L%, the last location in the array to be included in the sort.

Local variables: *left%*, the pointer at the lower end of the sub-array being sorted.

right%, the pointer at the upper end of the sub-array being sorted.

temporary, the variable used to hold a value while the values in two locations of the array are being swapped.

comparand, the comparand, a value taken from near the middle of the array or sub-array.

Actual parameters: *firstposition%*, *lastposition%*.

Global arrays: *sample*, holds the values to be sorted.

Listing:

```
 10  CLS
 20  DIM sample(10)
 30  firstposition%=1
 40  lastposition%=10
 50  PRINT "ENTER 10 NUMBERS IN MIXED O
RDER"
 60  FOR J=1 TO 10
 70    INPUT sample(J):NEXT
 80  PROCquicksortnumber(firstposition%
,lastposition%)
 90  PRINT "NUMBERS ARE NOW SORTED"
100  FOR J=1 TO 10:PRINTsample(J):NEXT
110  END
120  REM ************************
130  DEF PROCquicksortnumber(F%,L%)
140  LOCAL left%,right%,temporary,compa
rand
150  left%=F%:right%=L%:comparand=sampl
e((F%+L%)DIV2)
```

```
 160 REPEAT
 170    IF sample(left%)<comparand THEN
REPEAT:left%=left%+1:UNTIL sample(left%)
>=comparand
 180    IF comparand<sample(right%) THEN
 REPEAT right%=right%-1:UNTIL comparand>
=sample(right%)
 190    IF left%<=right% temporary=sampl
e(left%):sample(left%)=sample(right%):sa
mple(right%)=temporary:left%=left%+1:rig
ht%=right%-1
 200    UNTIL left%>right%
 210 IF F%<right% PROCquicksortnumber(F
%,right%)
 220 IF left%<L%PROCquicksortnumber(lef
t%,L%)
 230 ENDPROC
```

How it works: This procedure uses the standard quicksort algorithm. This is of interest as an example of a recursive procedure (lines 210 and 220).

Calling program: The program begins by dimensioning *sample*() to hold ten values. Quicksort can, of course, operate on far more values than this, at very high speed, but ten values are sufficient for the demonstration. Lines 30 and 40 assign values to *firstposition%* and *lastposition%* so that the whole array will be sorted. You are next asked to enter ten values for sorting. These may be positive or negative, integer or real. As soon as you have keyed in the numbers, the procedure is called to sort them (line 80). Line 100 displays the contents of the array after sorting. The numbers are in ascending numerical order.

The procedure need not necessarily sort all the numbers in the array, for its parameters set the first and last locations to be included in the sort. Values in different sections of the array can be sorted independently. The advantage of this is that the procedure may be used several times in a program to sort different sets of values held in different sections of the same array. At the beginning of the program, dimension *sample*() to make it large enough to hold all the sets of values that you will need to sort. As sets of values are derived in the program, store them in their particular sections of *sample*(). When any one set is to be sorted (without disturbing the other sets), call the procedure, using its parameters to specify which section of the array is to be sorted.

PROCquicksortword

What it does: Sorts, in alphabetical order, the contents of a string array.

Formal parameters: *F%*, the first location in the array to be included in the sort.
L%, the last location in the array to be included in the sort.

Local variables: *left%*, the pointer at the lower end of the sub-array being sorted.
right%, the pointer at the upper end of the sub-array being sorted.
temporary$, the variable used to hold a string while the values in two locations of the array are being swapped.
comparand$, the comparand, a string value taken from near the middle of the array or sub-array.

Actual parameters: *firstposition%, lastposition%*.

Global arrays: *sample$*, holds the strings to be sorted.

Listing:

```
 10 CLS
 20 DIM sample$(10)
 30 firstposition%=1
 40 lastposition%=10
 50 PRINT "ENTER 10 WORDS IN MIXED ORD
ER"
 60 FOR J=1 TO 10
 70   INPUT sample$(J):NEXT
 80 PROCquicksortword(firstposition%,l
astposition%)
 90 PRINT "WORDS ARE NOW SORTED"
100 FOR J=1 TO 10:PRINT;sample$(J):NEX
T
110 END
120 REM ************************
130 DEF PROCquicksortword(F%,L%)
140 LOCAL left%,right%,temporary$,comp
arand$
150 left%=F%:right%=L%:comparand$=samp
le$((F%+L%)DIV2)
```

```
 160 REPEAT
 170    IF sample$(left%)<comparand$ THE
N REPEAT:left%=left%+1:UNTIL sample$(lef
t%)>=comparand$
 180    IF comparand$<sample$(right%) TH
EN REPEAT right%=right%-1:UNTIL comparan
d$>=sample$(right%)
 190    IF left%<=right% temporary$=samp
le$(left%):sample$(left%)=sample$(right%
):sample$(right%)=temporary$:left%=left%
+1:right%=right%-1
 200    UNTIL left%>right%
 210 IF F%<right% PROCquicksortword(F%,
right%)
 220 IF left%<L% PROCquicksortword(left
%,L%)
 230 ENDPROC
```

How it works: This procedure uses the standard quicksort algorithm. Words are sorted according to the ASCII codes of the letters. This means that words should either be all in capitals (upper-case) or all in lower-case.

Calling program: The program begins by dimensioning *sample$* to hold ten words or phrases. Quicksort can, of course, operate on far more strings than this, at very high speed, but ten words are sufficient for the demonstration. Lines 30 and 40 assign values to *firstposition%* and *lastposition%* so that the whole array will be sorted. You are next asked to enter ten words (or phrases) for sorting. As soon as you have keyed in the words, the procedure is called to sort them (line 80). Line 100 displays the content of the array after sorting. The words are in alphabetical order.

The procedure need not necessarily sort all the words in the array, for its parameters set the first and last locations to be included in the sort. Words in different sections of the array can be sorted independently. The way to make use of this feature is described under PROCquicksortnumber. This routine is extremely fast but, in certain applications, it may be wasteful of memory. If the longest words or phrases are very long, while others are very short, or, if shortage of memory is likely to be a problem, (e.g. with large amounts of stored data, a long program, using Modes 0–3), it may be preferable to use PROCinsert and its associated procedures instead of PROCquicksortword.

PROCrectangle

What it does: Draws a rectangle of any size and colour.

Formal parameters: *C*, the colour.

a, distance in graphics units between the left side of the screen and the left side of the rectangle.

b, distance in graphics units between the bottom of the screen and the bottom of the rectangle.

c, distance in graphics units between the left side of the screen and the right side of the rectangle.

d, distance in graphics units between the bottom of the screen and the top of the rectangle.

Local variables: None.

Actual parameters: *colour, leftx, bottomy, rightx, topy.*

Listing:

```
 10 MODE 4
 20 INPUT "Left X "leftx
 30 INPUT "Right X "rightx
 40 INPUT "Bottom Y "bottomy
 50 INPUT "Top Y "topy
 60 INPUT "Select a colour "colour
 70 PROCrectangle(colour,leftx,bottomy
,rightx,topy)
 80 END
 90 REM ************************
100 DEF PROCrectangle(C,a,b,c,d)
110 GCOL 0,C
120 MOVE a,b:DRAW c,b:DRAW c,d:DRAW a,
d:DRAW a,b
130 ENDPROC
```

How it works: After setting the foreground colour, using GCOL (line 110), the procedure moves the graphics cursor to the bottom left corner of the rectangle, using MOVE (line 120). It then draws the rectangle by directing the cursor to each of the other three corners in turn, finally returning it to the bottom left corner (line 120).

Calling program: This procedure may be used in any graphics mode. The demonstration uses Mode 4, but you can alter line 10 to obtain other modes (see below). You are asked to key in the distances of the left and right sides from the left side of the screen. These are referred to as 'Left X' and 'Right X' in the input messages. Values of X should lie in the range 0 to 1279, with 'Right X' being greater than 'Left X'. Then you are asked to key in the distances of the bottom and top of the rectangle from the bottom of the screen, 'Bottom Y' and 'Top Y'. These values should lie in the range 0 to 1023, with 'Top Y' being greater than 'Bottom Y'.

Finally you are asked to key in a number to select the colour of the rectangle. Choose a number in these ranges:

Modes 0 and 4	1
Modes 1 and 5	1–3
Mode 2	1–15

Keying colour zero in any mode plots the rectangle in the background colour, so it is invisible! In your own programs you may find it useful to do this to delete a rectangle that has already been drawn.

As soon as all the details have been keyed in, the procedure is called and the rectangle appears on the screen. This is a very useful routine for producing 'boxes' for titles and for setting out tables for displaying information.

Associated routines: PROCsolidrectangle.

PROCreset

What it does: Resets certain functions within the computer to their normal operating mode.

Formal parameters: None.

Local variables: None.

Actual parameters: None.

Listing:
```
   10 CLS:VDU 23,68,196,71,69,127,124,12
4,72,108
   20 PRINT TAB(20,10)"D"
   30 *FX 4,1
   40 VDU 19,1,1,0,0,0,19,0,2,0,0,0
   50 PRINT "Press copy key to display 1
35":key=GET
   60 IF key=135 THEN PRINT "135"
   70 *FX 11,0
   80 INPUT "Press A and hold down "A
   90 SOUND 1,-15,4,-1:VDU 23,1,0;0;0;0;
  100 PRINT "Press any key to continue"
  110 key$=GET$:PROCreset
  120 PRINT TAB(20,16)"D"
  130 END
  140 REM ***********************
  150 DEF PROCreset
  160 *FX 4,0
  170 *FX 12,0
  180 *FX 15,0
  190 *FX 20,0
  200 VDU 23,1,1;0;0;0;20
  210 ENDPROC
```

How it works: Line 160 resets the COPY and cursor editing keys so that they perform their normal cursor editing function. Line 170 resets the auto-repeat function and resets the auto-repeat delay period to its normal length. Line 180 flushes all internal buffers (including the keyboard buffer and sound buffer). Line 190 causes the keyboard characters to be redefined to their usual form. Line 200 turns the cursor on; the final '20' restores the default colours (white text on black) except in Mode 7.

Calling program: The calling program puts the functions into their non-normal modes, and demonstrates their effects. Line 10 defines "D" as a 'dog', which is displayed at line 20. Line 30 disables the COPY key and the cursor editing keys. Line 40 gives red text on yellow, except in Mode 7. As a demonstration of key disabling, line 50 asks you to press the COPY key and waits for your key-press. When you press the COPY key, it generates its ASCII code (135) instead of performing its copy function. *Key* equals 135, and line 60 displays '135' to prove it. The cursor editing keys are affected in a similar way, though the calling program does not demonstrate this. Line 70 turns off the auto-repeat on all keys, after which line 80 invites you to press 'A' and hold it down.

You will find that only one 'A' is displayed; the key does not repeat. Press RETURN when you are satisfied that the auto-repeat is disabled. Immediately, a tone is heard. This continues indefinitely, unless stopped. You will also notice that the cursor is no longer flashing on the screen; it has been disabled by the VDU 23 statement in line 90. Line 100 invites you to press any key to continue and line 110 waits for the key-press. As soon as you press a key, the program calls the procedure, which restores everything to normal. Flushing the internal buffers stops the sound (among other things), and the cursor reappears next to the BASIC prompt mark. Everything on the screen is now black and white, and a letter 'D' is displayed by line 120. Press key 'A' now and it repeats automatically. Had the calling program altered the rate of repeat, this too would have been restored to normal. You will also find that the COPY and cursor editing keys behave in the normal way.

To sum up, this is a general-purpose procedure for restoring normal action to the computer. If certain functions have *not* been altered by the calling program, it does no harm to reset them. So this procedure may be called to reset any one of more of these functions.

PROCrightwrong

What it does: Validates single-key input, producing a sound to indicate if the key pressed is the right one or not.

Formal parameters: *R$*, the right key.

Local variables: *key$*, the key currently pressed.

Actual parameters: *response$*.

Listing:

```
  10 CLS
  20 INPUT "Select a key for right resp
onse "response$
  30 PRINT'"Any other key is wrong resp
onse"
  40 PROCrightwrong(response$)
  50 END
  60 REM ***********************
  70 DEF PROCrightwrong(R$)
  80 LOCAL key$
  90 REPEAT
```

```
   100    *FX 15,1
   110    key$=GET$
   120    IF key$<>R$ THEN SOUND 1,-15,5,1
0
   130    UNTIL key$=R$:SOUND 1,-15,193,10
   140 ENDPROC
```

How it works: The procedure consists of a REPEAT ... UNTIL loop. The *FX 15 statement (line 100) flushes the currently selected input buffer (i.e. the keyboard input buffer), so that any key-presses made before the start of the loop or during the previous repetition of the loop, are ignored. At line 110, *key$* is assigned the value of any key currently being pressed. If this is not the right key, line 120 produces a low-pitched tone. Line 130 tests *key$* to find out if the right key has been pressed. If it has, the loop ends and the second statement on line 130 produces a high-pitched sound. If the right key has not been pressed, the loop is repeated.

Calling program: You are asked in line 20 to decide which key is to be the right key. The message at line 30 tells you that any other key is a wrong key. The procedure is called. Every time you press a wrong key you hear the low-pitched tone. As soon as you press the right key, you hear a high-pitched tone. The computer returns from the procedure and the program ends.

PROCrotate

What it does: Displays a given character in any position on the screen, rotated a quarter-turn to the left.

Formal parameters: *C$*, the character.
  X and *Y*, the TAB coordinates.

Local variables: *J%* and *K%*, the loop indices.
  byte%, contains the bit-pattern for a row of the re-defined character.
  bit%, the value of a bit read from character ROM.

Actual parameters: *char$, tabx, taby.*

Listing:

```
 10  MODE 4
 20  INPUT "Character "char$
 30  INPUT "TAB X "tabx
 40  INPUT "TAB Y "taby
 50  CLS
 60  PROCrotate(char$,tabx,taby)
 70  END
 80  REM ***************************
 90  DEF PROCrotate(C$,X,Y)
100  LOCAL J%,K%,byte%,bit%
110  FOR J%=0 TO 7
120    byte%=0:FOR K%=0 TO 7
130      bit%=(?(&C000+8*(ASC(C$)-32)+K
%))AND2↑J%
140      IF bit%>0 THEN byte%=byte%+2↑(
7-K%)
150    NEXT
160    J%?3072=byte%
170  NEXT
180  PRINT TAB(X,Y)CHR$(224);
190  ENDPROC
```

How it works: The procedure reads bits from the character ROM and defines the user-definable character 224 in RAM to produce a rotated image of the original character. The problem is that a character is always defined by the *rows* of dots (pixels) of which it is composed. To create a rotated character we have to examine the definition of the original character in ROM and find out the arrangement of the dots by *columns*. The pattern so obtained must then be converted into a pattern by *rows* so that the rotated character may be defined in RAM.

The procedure uses two nested loops. The outer loop operates eight times, building up the 8 bytes (one at a time, in *byte%*) needed to define character 224. At the beginning of the outer loop, *byte%* is made zero (line 120) to clear it. At the end of the outer loop, the value of *byte%* is stored in RAM (addresses 3072 to 3079) where it defines the rotated character.

The inner loop calculates the successive values of *byte%*. It does this one bit at a time. The loop is repeated eight times, once for each of the bits in *byte%*. The eight bytes for the original character are stored in ROM from address &C000 onwards. There are groups of 8 bytes for each ASCII character. By using the ASCII code for *C$*, the location in ROM of the first of these bytes is calculated. Then, at each repetition of the loop, all eight bytes are tested to find the value of the corresponding bit in each byte. The first time round the outer loop ($J\%=0$), the value of bit 0 of each byte is found by ANDing the byte with 1 ($2^{\wedge}0$). The next time round ($J\%=1$), the value of bit 1 of each byte is found by ANDing with 2 ($2^{\wedge}1$), and so on for each bit. If a bit is found to have a value greater than 0, its value is added to *byte%* (line 140). As successive values of *byte%* are calculated, (first for all the bit zeros, then for all the bit 1s, then for all the bit 2s and so on up to all the bit 7s), it is used to define character 224. Finally, character 224 is displayed at the required TAB position.

Calling program: The program begins by putting the computer into Mode 4. The procedure works in any mode, except Mode 7. The details are then keyed in and the screen is cleared. PROCrotate then displays the rotated character where required.

Associated routines: PROCsideways.

PROCsave

What it does: Saves the contents of a block of memory on to disk or tape. The equivalent of the operating system statement *SAVE.

Formal parameters: *F$*, the file name.
 S$, the base (or start) address of the block of memory, in hexadecimal.
 L$, the length (number of bytes) to be saved, in hexadecimal.

Local variables: *B*, the length of the string to be stored in the file string buffer.
 fsbuffer, the base address of the file string buffer.

Actual parameters: *file$*, *start$*, *length$*.

Listing:

```
10 MODE 7
20 INPUT "Enter file name "file$
30 INPUT "Enter base address (hex) "s
tart$
40 INPUT "Enter length in bytes (hex)
"length$
```

```
  50 PRINT "Here it is"
  60 PROCsave(file$,start$,length$)
  70 END
  80 REM *************************
  90 DEF PROCsave(F$,S$,L$)
 100 LOCAL B,fsbuffer
 110 B=LEN(F$+S$+L$)+7
 120 DIM fsbuffer B-1
 130 X%=fsbuffer MOD 256:Y%=fsbuffer DI
V 256
 140 $fsbuffer="SAVE "+F$+" "+S$+" "+L
$
 150 CALL &FFF7
 160 ENDPROC
```

How it works: The file string buffer is to be filled with a string which is to be used as a command, sent to the command line interpreter routine (CLI). We must first calculate B, the length of this string. The string has the format

SAVE NAME SSSS LLLL

in which NAME is the file name under which the data is to be saved, SSSS is the base address and LLLL is the number of bytes to be saved. The length of this string is calculated in line 110, with 7 bytes added to allow for the word SAVE and the spaces required in the string. This done, a small block of memory (the file string buffer) is set aside in line 120 to hold the string. The value of *fsbuffer* is the base address of this block. This value is converted into two bytes and assigned to $X\%$ (low byte) and $Y\%$ (high byte) by line 130. The string indirection operator, ($), is used in line 140 to store the concatenated command string in the file string buffer. Line 150 calls the operating system command line interpreter routine (OSCLI). When this is done, the values of $X\%$ and $Y\%$ are automatically loaded into the X and Y registers of the microprocessor, so passing the address at which the command statement is to be found to the CLI routines. This statement is then executed and the content of the block of memory is saved on to disk or tape.

Calling program: The calling program puts the computer into Mode 7 for the purposes of the demonstration, though the procedure will work in any mode.

Before running the calling program, place a disk in the drive or, if you are using tapes, place a cassette, (wound to a suitable position), in the recorder.

Run the program and key in the file name under which the data is to be saved (not more than 7 characters, if you are using disks). Then key in the starting address and length (number of bytes) in hexadecimal, but not preceded by an '&'. For the demonstration, use the value 7C00 which is the base address of screen memory in Mode 7. To store the whole screen in Mode 7, the value to be keyed in for length is 03E8, the hexadecimal equivalent of 1000 decimal. As soon as you have entered these details, PROCsave is called. If you are using disks, the data will be saved automatically. If you are using tape, the message 'RECORD then RETURN' will be displayed. Press RECORD and PLAY on the recorder. Then press RETURN on the micro. The data will then be saved and the program ends.

Observe the screen carefully, so that you will be able to recall what is on it. This will reappear on the screen when you demonstrate PROCload.

Associated routines: PROCload.

PROCscrolldown

What it does: Scrolls the screen downward.

Formal parameters: *S*, the speed of scrolling.

Local variables: *J*, loop index for scrolling action.
  K, delay loop index.
  Y, the number of lines on the screen in the current mode.

Actual parameters: *speed*.

Listing:

```
10 CLS
20 INPUT "SPEED "speed
30 PROCscrolldown(speed)
40 END
50 REM ************************
60 DEF PROCscrolldown(S)
```

```
 70 LOCAL J,K,Y
 80 Y=INT(?&354*256/(?&352+256*?&353))
 90 FOR J=1 TO Y
100    FOR K=1 TO speed
110       NEXT
120    VDU 11
130    NEXT
140 ENDPROC
```

How it works: Line 80 finds out how many screen lines there are in the current mode. This is found by reading memory to find how many bytes are needed for storing the whole screen, and how many bytes are needed for storing a line. Dividing one value by the other gives the number of lines in the screen.

The loop in lines 90 to 130 begins with a delay loop (lines 100 to 110) nested within it. The length of the delay depends on the value of *S*. The greater its value, the longer the delay, and the slower the scrolling. After the delay, the VDU 11 statement at line 120 moves the cursor up one line. If the cursor is already on the top line of the screen, the effect is to scroll the whole screen display down one line. The loop is repeated once for each line on the screen.

Calling program: The only parameter to be set is the speed (line 20); enter a value between 5 and 500. The procedure is then called and the word SPEED, which was originally on the top line, scrolls down to the bottom line. If you modify the program by substituting an expression such as VDU 31,0,15 for the CLS in line 10, the cursor is half-way down the screen when you are asked to enter the speed. It is a good idea to run this amended demonstration with a screenful of text (e.g. a listing of the program) already there. After you have keyed in the speed, there is a delay while the cursor moves up to the top of the screen. Then the screenful of text scrolls down, until the word SPEED is in the bottom line.

Variations: If you intend to use this procedure on a dual-processor system, substitute this for line 80:

80   Y=FNvdupeek (&54)*256/FNvdudeek(&52)

Include FNvdupeek and FNvdudeek in the calling program.

PROCscrollside

What it does: Scrolls the screen sideways to the left, in any mode.

Formal parameters: *D%*, the distance the screen is to be scrolled.
S%, the speed of scrolling.

Local variables: *J*, the loop index.
line%, one eighth of the number of bytes required to store a line in the
current mode.
step%, the value by which the screen start register is incremented.

Actual parameters: *distance%, speed%.*

Listing:

```
  10 CLS
  20 INPUT "How far? "distance%
  30 INPUT "SPEED? "speed%
  40 CLS
  50 FOR J=0 TO 20
  60    PRINT TAB(J,J)STRING$(J,CHR$(J+
7))
  70    NEXT
  80 FOR J=1 TO 1500:NEXT
  90 PROCscrollside(distance%,speed%)
 100 END
 110 REM ************************
 120 DEF PROCscrollside(D%,S%)
 130 LOCAL J,line%,step%
 140 line%=(?&352+256*?&353)/8
 150 IF ?&34F=1 THEN line%=line%*8
 160 FOR J=0 TO D%
 170    step%=J MOD line%+8
 180    VDU 23;13,step%;0;0;0
 190    FOR K=1 TO S%:NEXT
 200    NEXT
```

How it works: The procedure operates by incrementing the low order
screen start address register (register 13), of the 6845 CRTC chip. Line
140 reads memory to find the number of bytes required to display a
screen line in the current mode. This value, when divided by 8 (the
number of bytes per character) gives *line%*, which equals the number of
characters per line in Modes 0, 3, 4 and 6. These are the two-colour

modes. In the four-colour modes and in Mode 2, the additional numbers of bytes needed to specify the colours are such that this value can be used as the basis for deciding when a whole line has been scrolled across. In Mode 7, the calculation is rather different, because colours are decided in that mode by control characters placed in video memory. Line 150 detects if Mode 7 is in operation and, if so, adjusts the value of *line%*.

The loop in lines 160 to 200 sends a succession of values to register 13 of the 6845. These are sent by the VDU command in line 180, in which *step%* is the value sent. The modular division in line 170 increments *step%* to a value determined by *line%*. The effect of this is that the screen scrolls its whole width as *step%* gradually increases and then returns to its original state when *step%* becomes zero again. The screen is actually scrolled across one complete width, then returned to its initial position and scrolled again. This technique avoids the upward scrolling that occurs when the screen is continuously scrolled sideways.

Line 190 provides the speed control. The greater the value of *S%* the longer the delay and the slower the scroll.

Calling program: Begin by putting the computer into any mode you choose. Line 20 asks you to specify the distance. To calculate this, consider the screen width to be 80 in Modes 0 to 3 and 40 in Modes 4 to 7. Calculate how many screen widths you want to scroll and multiply 40 or 80 by this number. Subtract 8 from the product and key in the result. Line 30 asks for speed. The fastest scrolling (which is *very fast*) is obtained by keying 1. For a more leisurely scroll, which gives you time to read the text as it scrolls by, key in a larger number such as 100 or 200.

The screen clears to produce a display of characters. There is a short pause to allow you to see them, (line 80), and then the procedure scrolls the screen.

Variations: If you intend to use this program on a dual processor system, substitute these lines for lines 140 and 150:

```
140 line%=FNvdudeek(&52)/8
150 IF FNvdupeek(&4F)=1 THEN line %=line%*8
```

Include FNvdudeek and FNvdupeek in the calling program.

PROCselectanumber

What it does: Accepts numeric input within a specified range of values.

Formal parameters: $M\$$, a message to be displayed when input is required.
   L, the lower limit for the number.
   U, the upper limit for the number.

Local variables: $number\$$, the number, as a string.

Actual parameters: $message\$$, min, max.

Global variables: $number$, the number being keyed in.

Listing:

```
 10 CLS
 20 INPUT "Message "message$
 30 INPUT "Min "min
 40 INPUT "Max "max
 50 PROCselectanumber(message$,min,max
)
 60 CLS
 70 PRINT;number;" is the number"
 80 END
 90 REM *************************
100 DEF PROCselectanumber(M$,L,U)
110 LOCAL number$
120 REPEAT
130    CLS
140    PRINT M$" ";L;" TO ";U;
150    INPUT" "number$:number=VAL(numbe
r$)
160    VDU 13,11
170 UNTIL number>=L AND number<=U AN
D NOT (number=0 AND LEFT$(number$,1)<>"0
")
180 ENDPROC
```

How it works: The action of the procedure is contained in a REPEAT … UNTIL loop, lines 120 to 170. The screen is cleared, (or just one line or a part of the screen can be cleared; see the variations described later), and the prompt or query message is displayed. This indicates the lower and upper limits of acceptable values. Line 150 waits for input from the user. This is accepted as a string and converted into a value which is assigned to *number*.

Line 160 returns the cursor to the beginning of the line the message is displayed on, ready for repeating the INPUT statement should an out-of-range response be made. Line 170 makes the loop repeat until *number* is equal to, or lies between, the lower and upper limits. There is a further condition in line 170 which deals with instances in which the user may have typed letters of the alphabet instead of numerals. If *number$* begins with a letter or symbol, VAL assigns zero value to *number*. The final condition in line 170 makes the loop repeat if *number* equals zero but the first character keyed in was not zero. This explains why we use string input in line 150. Had we used *number* to receive the input instead of using *number$*, it would have become equal to zero when a letter was typed in. But it would then not be possible to know at line 170 if the zero value of *number* was due to a letter or a zero.

Calling program: Lines 20 to 40 ask you to key in a query message (e.g. 'What month is it (1–12)'), and the minimum and maximum values that are acceptable as input (e.g. 1 and 12). Then the procedure is called, the screen is cleared and the message is displayed. The computer waits until you have keyed in an acceptable value. If the number is accepted, the computer returns to the calling program and displays it. If not, it clears the screen, re-displays the message and waits for a correct response.

Variations: In some applications you may prefer to clear only part of the screen or perhaps only the line that the message is on when an incorrect response is made. Instead of the CLS in line 130, use PROCclearscreen or PROCblankline, and include the appropriate procedure in the calling program. In PROCclearscreen omit the −1 from lines 110 and 160. In PROCblankline omit the comma and the '11' from line 90.

Associated routines: FNacceptletter.

PROCsideways

What it does: Displays a given string so that it reads vertically from bottom to top, as required, for labelling the vertical axis of a graph or a narrow column in a table.

Formal parameters: *M$*, the string to be displayed.

X, the horizontal coordinate of the string when displayed.

Y, the vertical coordinate of the lowermost character of the string when displayed.

Local variables: *J*, loop index.

Actual parameters: *message$*, *tabx*, *taby*.

Listing:

```
 10 MODE 4
 20 INPUT LINE "Message "message$
 30 INPUT "TAB X "tabx
 40 INPUT "TAB Y "taby
 50 CLS
 60 PROCsideways(message$,tabx,taby)
 70 END
 80 DEF PROCrotate(C$,X,Y)
 90 LOCAL J%,K%,byte%,bit%
100 FOR J%=0 TO 7
110    byte%=0:FOR K%=0 TO 7
120       bit%=(?(&C000+8*(ASC(C$)-32)+K
%))AND2^J%
130       IF bit%>0 THEN byte%=byte%+2^(
7-K%)
140       NEXT
150    J%?3072=byte%
160    NEXT
170 PRINT TAB(X,Y)CHR$(224);
180 ENDPROC
190 REM ***************************
200 DEFPROCsideways(M$,X,Y)
210 LOCAL J
220 VDU 23,1,0;0;0;0;
230 FOR J=1 TO LEN(M$)
240    PROCrotate(MID$(M$,J,1),X,Y-J+1)
250    NEXT
260 VDU 31,0,Y+1
270 VDU 23,1,1;0;0;0;
280 ENDPROC
```

How it works: Line 220 disables the cursor, to prevent it from spoiling any display that may already exist when the procedure is called (the calling program clears the screen before calling the procedure but it is not essential to do this). Lines 230 to 250 take each letter of the message in turn and call PROCrotate to display it in rotated form. The first letter is displayed at TAB(X,Y) and subsequent letters are displayed in a vertical column upwards from that point. Line 260 brings the cursor to the left-hand end of the row below the lower end of the displayed message, and then line 270 turns the cursor on again.

Calling program: This begins by putting the computer into Mode 4. The procedure works in any mode except Mode 7. The use of INPUT LINE in line 20 allows you to key in a string which contains commas, if you wish. Then key in the TAB position of the *lower* end of the column. X can have any value between 0 and 39 in Mode 4, and also in Modes 1 and 6. In Modes 0 and 3 its maximum value is 79, while in Modes 2 and 5 it is 19. Y can have any value from 0 to 31 in Modes 0, 1, 2, 4, and 5. In Modes 3 and 6 the maximum value is 24. However, make sure that the value of Y is sufficiently large to allow the column to be built up from that level.

Associated routines: PROCrotate.

PROCsolidpolygon

What it does: Draws a polygon with solid colour.

Formal parameters: C, the colour of the polygon.
  N, the number of sides of the polygon.

Local variables: J, the loop index.

Actual parameters: *colour*, *sides*.

Global arrays: *polygon*, the graphics coordinates of the corners of the polygon.

Listing:

```
10 MODE 4
20 DIM polygon(15,1)
30 INPUT "How many sides (3-15) "side
s
```

```
  40 PRINT "Key X and Y coordinates"
  50 FOR J=1 TO sides
  60    PRINT "Corner ";J;:INPUT " "poly
gon(J,0),polygon(J,1)
  70    NEXT
  80 INPUT "Select a colour "colour
  90 MODE 2
 100 PROCsolidpolygon(colour,sides)
 110 END
 120 REM ************************
 130 DEF PROCsolidpolygon(C,N)
 140 LOCAL J
 150 GCOL 0,C
 160 FOR J=2 TO N-1
 170    MOVE polygon(1,0),polygon(1,1)
 180    MOVE polygon(J,0),polygon(J,1)
 190    PLOT 85,polygon(J+1,0),polygon(J
+1,1)
 200    NEXT
 210 ENDPROC
```

How it works: The procedure draws and fills a number of triangles, to make up the polygon. The graphics cursor is moved to the position of the first corner (line 170). Then a number of triangles (two fewer than the number of sides of the polygon) are drawn, using PLOT 85 (line 190). All triangles begin at the first corner of the polygon. The loop (lines 160 to 200) works systematically around the polygon drawing triangles which include successive pairs of sides of the polygon.

Calling program: The array dimensioned in line 20 allows for the polygon to have up to 15 sides. You need not alter this for polygons with fewer than 15 sides. If you wish to draw polygons with more than 15 sides, increase the 15 in line 20 accordingly. You are asked how many sides you require, and then for the X and Y coordinates. Key in the coordinates as a pair of values, separated by a comma. These coordinates are the ordinary graphics coordinates ranging from 0 to 1279 for X and 0 to 1023 for Y, as explained in Chapter 8 of the User Guide. As you enter each pair of values the X coordinate is stored in *polygon* (*J*,0) and the Y coordinate is stored in *polygon* (*J*,1)'.

The value that you can enter for colour depends on which mode the computer is in. The calling program puts the computer into Mode 2 (line 90) before calling the procedure, but you can substitute any other graphics mode for this. (Note that the program begins by putting the computer into Mode 4, to make it easier to read the input messages after having been in Mode 2.) The range of values input for the colour should be:

Modes 0 and 4   1
Modes 1 and 5   1–3
Mode 2   1–15

Entering zero in any mode gives an invisible polygon in background colour! This technique can be used (in your own programs) for deleting a polygon which has already been drawn.

This is a very fast routine, but has one limitation. The polygon is not properly drawn unless every corner can be 'seen' from the first corner of the polygon. That is to say, a line joining the first corner with another corner must not cut across any of the intended sides of the polygon. This means that it may not draw a polygon correctly if it is very irregular in shape, with many sharply re-entrant angles. However, even in these unlikely instances, drawing out the polygon on graph paper beforehand can help. You may be able to find a corner from which all the others can be 'seen'. Begin at this corner when entering the coordinates.

Associated routines: PROCpolygon.

PROCsolidrectangle

What it does: Draws a rectangle of any size, filled with a selected colour.

Formal parameters: a, distance in graphics units between the left side of the screen and the left side of the rectangle.

b, distance in graphics units between the bottom of the screen and the bottom of the rectangle.

c, distance in graphics units between the left side of the screen and the right side of the rectangle.

d, distance in graphics units between the bottom of the screen and the top of the rectangle.

C, the colour.

Local variables: None.

Actual parameters: *leftx, bottomy, rightx, topy, colour.*

Listing:

```
 10 MODE 4
 20 INPUT "Left X "leftx
 30 INPUT "Right X "rightx
 40 INPUT "Bottom Y "bottomy
 50 INPUT "Top Y "topy
 60 INPUT "Select a colour "colour
 70 PROCsolidrectangle(leftx,bottomy,r
ightx,topy,colour)
 80 END
 90 REM ************************
100 DEF PROCsolidrectangle(a,b,c,d,C)
110 VDU 24,a;b;c;d;
120 GCOL 0,C:CLG
130 VDU 26
140 ENDPROC
```

How it works: The procedure draws the rectangle by setting up a graphics screen (or 'window') of the required size within the whole screen area. The VDU 24 statement in line 110 uses the four parameters *a, b, c* and *d* to define the window, as explained in Chapter 8 of the User Guide. The graphics background colour is set in line 120. The graphics screen is then cleared and takes the new background colour. Finally, the VDU 26 statement in line 130 restores the default windows. That is to say, the text and graphics windows now extend over the whole screen, the text cursor is returned to the top left corner and the graphics cursor is returned to the bottom left corner. In this way the procedure leaves the screen ready for text or graphics to be displayed anywhere on it.

Calling program: This procedure may be used in any graphics mode. The demonstration uses Mode 4, but you can alter line 10 to obtain other modes (see below).

You are asked to key in the distances of the left and right side from the left side of the screen. These are referred to as 'Left X' and 'Right X' in the input messages. Values of X should lie in the range 0 to 1279, with 'Right X' being greater than 'Left X'. Then you are asked to key in the distances of the bottom and top of the rectangle from the bottom of the screen, 'Bottom Y' and 'Top Y'. These values should lie in the range 0 to 1023, with 'TopY' being greater than 'Bottom Y'.

Finally you are asked to key in a number to select the colour of the rectangle. Choose a number in these ranges:

Modes 0 and 4   129
Modes 1 and 5   129–131
Mode 2   129–143

Keying colour 128 in any mode plots the rectangle in the current background colour, so it is invisible! In your own programs you may find it useful to do this to delete a rectangle that has already been drawn.

As soon as all details have been keyed in, the procedure is called and the rectangle appears on the screen.

Associated routines: PROCrectangle.

PROCspacecraft

What it does: Produces the sound of a spacecraft in flight.

Formal parameters: None.

Local variables: None.

Actual parameters: None.

Listing:

```
 10 PROCspacecraft
 20 END
 30 REM ************************
 40 DEF PROCspacecraft
 50 ENVELOPE 1,1,-8,8,0,10,10,0,126,0,
0,-126,126,126
 60 SOUND 1,1,150,254
 70 ENDPROC
```

How it works: Line 50 defines ENVELOPE 1 with the shortest possible step length (1). The parameters −8,8,0 produce a pitch that falls in section 1 and rises at an equal rate in section 2. The parameters 10,10,0 make sections 1 and 2 ten steps long, and there is no third phase. The overall effect of the pitch parameters is to produce a regular and repeated fall and rise of pitch. Attack is at maximum rate (126), so the sound begins at maximum volume. Amplitude is held constant during the decay and sustain phases (0,0). It falls sharply (−126) during the release phase. Target levels are set high (126,126) to maintain maximum volume.

The SOUND statement at line 60 uses a tone channel (channel 1) and ENVELOPE 1 (just defined). The pitch is fairly high (150) and the duration is just over 12 seconds (254).

Calling program: When the program is run, the procedure is called and the sound is heard. In your own programs it is a good idea to reserve ENVELOPE 1 for this procedure and for any other sound-effects procedures that may be used. Then ENVELOPE 1 is redefined each time one of these procedures is called. The other envelopes may then be defined globally at the beginning of the program to provide for musical tones and tunes.

Variations: To produce the sounds of different kinds of spacecraft, try altering the pitch of the SOUND command; change the 150 in line 60 to any other value between 0 and 254. If you want the sound to continue indefinitely, instead of lasting for only 12 seconds, change the 254 in line 60 to −1. You can also get different kinds of spacecraft noise by altering the envelope. Experiment with changing the amount by which pitch rises and falls (e.g. change −8 and 8 to −20 and 20), and the number of steps of rise and fall (e.g. alter the 10s to 20s).

PROCtable

What it does: Formats a table of data to fill the width of the screen.

Formal parameters: C, the number of columns.
  T, the total number of items of data in the table.

Local variables: X, the number of characters in a line in the current mode.
  chars, the number of characters in each column of the table.
  J, the loop counter.
  cells, the number of cells (i.e. items of data) that have been displayed at any given stage in the procedure.

Actual parameters: *columns, totalitems.*

Global arrays: *heading$,* contains the headings of the columns.
items, contains the data items.

Listing:

```
  10 CLS
  20 INPUT "Enter the number of columns
"columns
  30 INPUT "Enter the total number of i
tems "totalitems
  40 DIM heading$(columns),items(totali
tems+columns)
  50 PRINT "Enter ";columns" headings"
  60 FOR J=0 TO columns-1
  70    INPUT heading$(J)
  80    NEXT
  90 PRINT "Enter ";totalitems" items"
 100 FOR J=0 TO totalitems-1
 110    INPUT items(J)
 120    NEXT
 130 CLS
 140 PROCtable(columns,totalitems)
 150 END
 160 REM ****************************
 170 DEFPROCtable(C,T)
 180 LOCAL X,chars,J,cells
 190 X=(?&352+256*?&353)/?&34F
 200 chars=X DIV C
 210 FOR J=0 TO C-1
 220    PRINT TAB(J*chars)heading$(J);
 230    NEXT
 240 PRINT''
 250 REPEAT
 260    FOR J=cells TO cells+C-1
 270       PRINT TAB((J-cells)*chars);ite
ms(J);
 280       NEXT
 290    cells=cells+C
 300    UNTIL cells>=T
 310 ENDPROC
```

How it works: Line 190 reads memory to find out the number of bytes needed to store a single character. Dividing one value by the other gives *X*. The number of characters in a column is found in line 200. The column headings are displayed by the loop of lines 210 to 230. These are TABbed, being spaced *chars* spaces apart. Line 240 then prints two blank lines to separate the headings from the data.

The data is displayed by the routine of lines 250 to 300. This is a REPEAT ... UNTIL loop with a FOR ... NEXT loop nested inside it. The FOR ... NEXT loop displays a single line of the table, spacing them *chars* spaces apart. On the first time through the loop, *cells* equals 0, so the data is taken from location 0 to *C*–1 of *items*(). This displays a value in each of the *C* columns. Line 290 then increments *cells* by the number of columns, so that the appropriate batch of values is taken on each repeat of the FOR ... NEXT loop. After each repetition of the loop, *cells* holds the total number of items displayed so far. The conditions following UNTIL at line 300 send the computer back to display another line until the number of cells displayed is equal to, or greater than, the number of items in the table. If there are insufficient items to fill all columns equally, zeros are displayed in the unfilled places in the bottom line of the table.

Calling program: First of all, enter the number of columns the table is to have. Then enter the total number of items in the table; this need not be a multiple of the number of columns. The program then dimensions the arrays to hold column headings and the data items (line 40). Array *items*() is dimensioned with *columns* additional locations, to allow for the possibility of having to display zeros in the bottom line of the table.

Now a loop (lines 60 to 80) asks for the column headings to be typed in. The headings are automatically TABbed to start at the left of each column. Limit the length of these so that they will fit in the column width. For example, if there are 6 columns in a 40-column mode, the column width is 6 characters, and the headings must not be more than 5 characters long. This allows for a space between adjacent headings. Next you are asked to type in the data items (lines 90 to 120). Type these in the order in which they would be read from the table, reading across the lines of the table from left to right, and working from the top to the bottom of the table. As with the headings, the numbers must not have too many characters in them. With a column width of 6 characters, for example, the longest numbers you can enter are 12345, 123.4, 12.34, etc. As soon as all the items have been entered, the screen clears (line 130), PROCtable is called and the table is displayed.

Variations: If you intend to use this procedure on a dual processor system, substitute this line for line 190:

190 X=FNvdudeek(&52)/FNvdupeek(&4F)

Include FNvdudeek and FNvdupeek in the calling program.

PROCtelescreen

What it does: Creates a Teletext screen (Mode 7 only) in any required colour, with a different colour for the top (title) line. This can be repeatedly used for text or Teletext graphics displays without needing to use the Mode 7 colour codes for each line on the screen and for each new display.

Formal parameters: *TB*, the background colour for the title line.
   TF, the foreground colour for the title line.
   B, the background colour for the remainder of the screen.
   F, the foreground colour for the remainder of the screen.

Local variables: *Y*, the loop counter.

Actual parameters: *titlebg, titlefg, bg, fg*.

Listing:

```
   10 MODE 7
   20 INPUT "ENTER THE TITLE BACKGROUND
COLOUR "titlebg
   30 INPUT "ENTER THE TITLE FOREGROUND
COLOUR "titlefg
   40 INPUT "ENTER THE BACKGROUND COLOUR
 "bg
   50 INPUT "ENTER THE FOREGROUND COLOUR
 "fg
   60 PROCtelescreen(titlebg,titlefg,bg,
fg)
   70 PRINT "         THIS IS THE TITLE"
   80 PRINT "THIS IS THE TEXT------------
------"
   90 END
  100 REM ************************
```

```
110 DEF PROCtelescreen(TB,TF,B,F)
120 LOCAL Y
130 CLS
140 VDU TB,157,TF,13,10
150 FOR Y=0 TO 22
160    VDU B,157,F,13,10
170    NEXT
180 VDU B,157,F,30
190 VDU 28,3,24,39,0
200 ENDPROC
```

How it works: After clearing the screen, the procedure places Teletext colour codes at the extreme left of each line of the screen. Line 140 uses a VDU command to place the codes for the top line, or title line, which has different colours to allow it to give emphasis to the titles of displays. The action of the parameters of the VDU command are:

TB	select a background colour *TB*
157	declare *TB* to be the new background colour
TF	reselect the colour of the letters (foreground colour)
13	move cursor to beginning of line (carriage return)
10	move cursor down one line (line feed)

The loop in lines 150 to 170 performs a similar operation at the left of each of the other lines of the screen, except for the bottom line. The only difference is that the VDU statement in line 160 uses the values *B* and *F*. Line 180 similarly places colour codes on the bottom line of the screen, but does not effect a line feed.

The colour codes are now in place for every line of the screen, occupying the first three character positions on each. Line 190 uses the VDU 28 statement to define a text window that covers the whole screen except for the three columns on the left. This 'masks off' the colour codes so that they are not removed when the screen is cleared and are not changed in any way by anything that may subsequently be displayed on the screen. As far as handling the screen is concerned, these three columns are not there – you simply have a screen which is only 37 characters wide instead of 40. But as far as Mode 7 is concerned they *are* there, and they determine the foreground and background colours for each line of the screen.

Calling program: You are asked to key in the codes for the foreground and background colours of the title and the remainder of the screen. If for example, you want the title to be in yellow letters on a blue background, with the remainder of the screen in white letters on a red background, key in 131,132,129 and 135, in that order. The other codes that may be used are 130 for green, 133 for magenta, and 134 for cyan.

As soon as you have done this, the screen clears. The message 'THIS IS THE TITLE' appears in the chosen colours on the top line of the screen. The remainder of the screen changes colour and the message 'THIS IS THE TEXT-----' is displayed there.

Once a Mode 7 screen has been set up in this way, it can be used without further need to bother with colour codes.

Variations: The procedure can be adapted to produce bands of different colours at other positions on the screen. For example the bottom 3 or 4 lines could be reserved for displaying questions and prompt messages in colours different from those used on the remainder of the screen.

PROCtimer

What it does: Displays elapsed time in minutes and seconds.

Formal parameters: *T*, the initial value of *TIME*, the BBC Micro's pseudo variable, at the beginning of the timed period.

Local variables: *elapsedtime*, the elapsed time in hundredths of a second.
secs, the seconds portion of the elapsed time.
mins, the number of completed minutes in the elapsed time.

Actual parameters: *time*.

Listing:

```
10 CLS
20 time=TIME
30 FOR J=1 TO 100000:NEXT J
40 PROCtimer(time)
50 END
60 REM *************************
70 DEFPROCtimer(T)
80 LOCAL elapsedtime,secs,mins
```

```
 90 elapsedtime=(TIME-T)
100 secs=(elapsedtime DIV 100)MOD 60
110 mins=elapsedtime DIV 6000
120 PRINT TAB(24,1);mins" min ";secs"
sec "
130 ENDPROC
```

How it works: Line 90 calculates the elapsed time by subtracting T (the initial value of *TIME*) from the value of *TIME* at the instant the procedure is called. Line 100 divides *elapsedtime* by 100, to convert it from hundredths of a second to seconds. Then the MOD function is used to divide this result by 60. MOD returns a value between 0 and 59 (the remainder from the division) which represents the number of seconds left, after discounting those which make up completed minutes.

Line 110 converts *elapsedtime* into an integral number of minutes, using the DIV operator. Finally, line 120 displays the results of the calculations at the top right corner of the screen.

Calling program: Line 20 registers the time (the value of *TIME*) when the calling program is run. The screen remains blank for just over a minute because of the delay loop of line 30. As soon as the loop is finished, PROCtimer is called to display the time that has elapsed since the program began. Try altering the 100000 in line 30 to obtain elapsed times of differing lengths.

When using this procedure in your own programs, set *time* equal to *TIME* at that stage in the program from which all elapsed times are to be measured. The procedure may be called as often as you wish and will return the time elapsed on each occasion, counting from the starting time. Using this procedure does not interfere with the action of other procedures or routines which make use of *TIME*. However, if *TIME* is reset by other procedures, or in the main program, the result given by PROCtimer is certain to be affected. If you are using other timing routines in the same program, design them in a similar way to this procedure, so that they do not depend on resetting *TIME*.

Variations: The values used in the TAB statement of line 120 may be altered to display the time in any other position on the screen.

PROCtravellingtitle

What it does: Displays a title or other piece of text moving from left to right across any portion of the screen.

Formal parameters: *X*, initially, the first X position for the left-hand end of the title, then the current X position.
   Y, the current Y position for the title .
   T$, the title.
   S, the speed at which the title is to move.
   Z, the final X position for the right-hand end of the title.

Local variables: *T*, the delay loop index.

Actual parameters: *startx, taby, title$, speed, finishx.*

Listing:

```
 10 CLS
 20 INPUT "Enter the title "title$
 30 INPUT "Enter the Y coordinate "tab
y
 40 INPUT "Enter the speed "speed
 50 INPUT "Start,X = "startx
 60 INPUT "Finish,X = "finishx
 70 PROCtravellingtitle(startx,taby,ti
tle$,speed,finishx)
 80 END
 90 REM ************************
100 DEFPROCtravellingtitle(X,Y,T$,S,Z)
110 LOCAL T
120 CLS
130 REPEAT
140    PRINT TAB(X,Y)" "T$
150    X=X+1
160    FOR T=1 TO S:NEXT
170    UNTIL X=Z-LEN(T$)
180 ENDPROC
```

How it works: The action is contained in a REPEAT ... UNTIL loop. First the title is displayed, in its starting position, preceded by a blank space. Then *X* is incremented by 1, so that, on the next repetition of the loop, the blank space and title are displaced 1 position to the right. The space blanks out the first letter of the title previously displayed and the new title display replaces the remainder. There is a short delay at line 160 to allow time for the title to be seen in each position. The result is that the title appears to move sideways across the screen. The length of the delay determines its speed of progression. The greater the value of *S*, the longer the delay and the more slowly the title moves.

The loop repeats until the right-hand end of the title reaches the specified finishing position.

Calling program: The calling program asks you to key in the title, its Y coordinate (i.e. how many lines down the screen), its speed and its start and finishing positions. A suitable value for speed is 200, though it can range from about 50 to about 500. As soon as all details have been entered, the procedure is called and the title travels across the screen.

PROCtune

What it does: Plays a sequence of notes, determined by the composition of two strings.

Formal parameters: *N$*, the string which specifies the pitch of each note.

D$, the string which specifies the duration of each note.

flag%, determines whether or not the procedure waits for the tune to be played before returning to the main program.

Local variables: *J*, loop index.

note%, initially, the number of notes between the bottom of the scale and the current note; later, the number of semitones above the bottom of the scale.

Actual parameters: *note$*, *duration$*, *wait%*.

Listing:

```
10 INPUT "Notes      "note$
20 INPUT "Durations "duration$
30 INPUT "Wait or not (1 or 0) "wait%
40 PROCtune(note$,duration$,wait%)
50 END
```

```
  60 REM *************************
  70 DEF PROCtune(N$,D$,flag%)
  80 LOCAL J%,note%
  90 FOR J%=1 TO LEN(N$)
 100    note%=ASC(MID$(N$,J%,1))-65
 110    IF note%>6 THEN note%=note%-25
 120    IF note%>0 THEN note%=note%+1
 130    IF note%>3 THEN note%=note%+1
 140    IF note%>5 THEN note%=note%+1
 150    IF note%>8 THEN note%=note%+1
 160    IF note%>10 THEN note%=note%+1
 170    IF note%>12 THEN note%=note%+1
 180    IF note%>15 THEN note%=note%+1
 190    IF note%>17 THEN note%=note%+1
 200    IF note%>20 THEN note%=note%+1
 210    IF note%=-17 THEN SOUND 1,0,0,VA
L(MID$(D$,J%,1)) ELSE SOUND 1,-15,89+4*n
ote%,VAL(MID$(D$,J%,1))
 220    SOUND 1,0,0,1
 230    NEXT
 240 REPEAT UNTIL flag%=0 OR ADVAL(-6)=
15
 250 ENDPROC
```

How it works: The loop extending from lines 90 to 230 takes the notes one at a time and sends them to the sound buffer. Each note is read from *N$* by first finding its ASCII code and subtracting 65 (line 100). This gives the notes A to G the values 0 to 6, and the notes of the second octave, (represented by letters a to g), the values 32 to 38.

At line 110, the values corresponding to the second octave are reduced by 25. The result of this is that the values of *note%* now range in steps of 1, from 0 for the lower A to 13 for the upper g. Lines 120 to 200 work up the scales, incrementing the value of *note%* to take account of the fact that some adjacent notes are separated by whole tones, while others are separated only by semitones. When this operation is complete, *note%* is the number of semitones between each note and the lower A. Line 210 detects if the string contains a zero. If so a period of silence is sent to the sound buffer. If not, a note of the required pitch is sent. The procedure uses channel 1, at maximum volume. The third sound parameter (pitch) should be 89 for the lower A and be increased by 4 for each semitone above A. The expression given as the third parameter calculates the required value. The fourth sound parameter (duration) is obtained by reading the corresponding numeric character from *D$* and evaluating it.

Line 220 sends a short period of silence to the sound buffer, so that if two consecutive notes have the same pitch, they will not be run into one longer note.

The tune is heard as soon as the first note has been sent to the sound buffer. The loop sends notes faster than they can be played so the loop is finished before the whole of the tune has been heard.

Line 240 allows a return to the main program if *flag%* is zero (no wait). If 'flag%' is 1, there is a delay until ADVAL (−6) becomes 15, showing that the sound buffer for channel 1 is empty; in other words, that the tune has finished.

Note that if the tune is longer than can be accommodated in the sound buffer, the procedure waits for notes to be played to make room in the buffer. Then it sends the next batch of notes to the buffer. Thus it cannot send a complete long tune to the buffer and return immediately to the calling program. One advantage of this is that the maximum length of the tune is not limited by the size of the sound buffer but by the maximum length allowed for a string. This is 255 characters, allowing a very long tune to be played.

Calling program: The program first asks you to input the notes. Type in a string, using the letters A to G to represent the notes of the lower octave and a to g to represent the upper octave. Use a zero to represent a rest (silence). Do not include spaces or other characters in the string. An example of a tuneful string is 'CEDFEGEC'.

Next you are asked to key in the durations. Key in a string of digits (1–9), equal in length to the note string. A suitable string for the tune given above is '63633336'. The INPUT statements are arranged so that the value for the duration of each note is typed directly below the letter. When keying in the program, type 5 blank spaces after 'Notes' and one after 'Durations'.

Finally, you are asked whether or not the procedure is to wait for the tune to finish before returning to the calling program – key 1 or 0. There is not much point in this in the context of the calling program but, when you come to use the procedure in your own programs, this feature could be useful. For example, if you want a tune to be played while a game is in progress, you will probably want the procedure to feed the tune to the sound buffer and then return to the main program so that the action of the game can continue while the tune is being heard. On other occasions, perhaps in a musical program, you may want the complete tune to be heard before the program continues.

This procedure allows you to program the computer to play many different tunes at different stages in a program, simply by setting up two strings for each. The calling program does not allow the maximum number of notes to be played as it is not possible to build up a string 255 characters long when using INPUT. The maximum possible with the calling program is 238. However, in your own programs you can use full-length strings as actual parameters when calling the procedure. You are limited to about 231 by the maximum length of a program line. If you want a full length string, make up two strings and join them, using a statement such as 'note$=first$+second$', to make a string up to 255 characters long.

Variations: You could define an envelope at the beginning of the main program and make the sound statement of line 210 use this envelope. In this way you could make the tune sound as if it is being played by a musical instrument. As a further refinement of the procedure, you could add a fourth parameter to its definition, for selecting the envelope. You could then define several different envelopes at the beginning of the program and, when calling the procedure, specify which envelope was to be used.

PROCunderline

What it does: Displays underlined text in any given screen position.

Formal parameters: *X*, *Y*, the TAB positions for the beginning of the text.
   T$, the text.

Local variables: None.

Actual parameters: *tabx, taby, text$*.

Listing:

```
10 CLS
20 INPUT "Enter the X coordinate "ta
bx
30 INPUT "Enter the Y coordinate "tab
y
```

```
 40 INPUT "Enter the text "text$
 50 PROCunderline(tabx,taby,text$)
 60 END
 70 REM ***********************
 80 DEF PROCunderline(X,Y,T$)
 90 PRINT TAB(X,Y)T$
100 VDU 31,X,Y,10
110 PRINT STRING$(LEN(T$),"←")
120 ENDPROC
```

The left-arrow (←) in line 110 represents the 'underline' character on the BBC Micro.

How it works: Line 90 displays the text in the required position. Line 100 positions the cursor on the line below, ready to display the underlining. In Modes 0 to 6, line 110 displays a string of 'underline' characters, equal in length to the text. In Mode 7 the equivalent character produces a dashed line instead of a continuous one.

Calling program: Key in the X and Y coordinates. The minimum value of either is 0, and the maximum values depend on the current mode. Key in the text. Note that the length of the text and the value of X must be such that the text is all on one screen line. PROCunderline then displays the text in the required position, underlined.

PROCwait

What it does: A dual-purpose input routine which makes the computer *either:* wait indefinitely until a specified key is pressed; *or,* wait until any key is pressed or a specified time has elapsed, whichever happens first.

Formal parameters: *K$*, the character of the specified key.
   T, the specified waiting time, in hundredths of a second.

Local variables: *key$*, the character of the pressed key.

Actual parameters: *response$, period.*

Listing:

```
 10 CLS
 20 INPUT "Press specified key "respon
se$
 30 INPUT "Wait specified time "period
 40 PROCwait(response$,period)
 50 PRINT "Finished"
 60 END
 70 REM ***************************
 80 DEF PROCwait(K$,T)
 90 LOCAL key$
100 REPEAT
110   *FX 15,1
120   key$=INKEY$(T)
130   UNTIL key$=K$ OR T>0
140 ENDPROC
```

How it works: The procedure consists of a REPEAT ... UNTIL loop. The *FX 15 call on line 110 flushes the currently selected input buffer, (i.e. the keyboard input buffer), so that any key-presses made before the start of the loop or during the previous repetition of the loop, are ignored. Line 120 uses INKEY$ which waits until a key is pressed or a given period of time has elapsed before continuing. The length of time it waits depends on the value of the parameter of INKEY$ which, in this procedure is the value of *T*.

The procedure may be used in one of two different ways:
1) With *K$* having the value of one of the characters of the keyboard and *T* being equal to zero.
2) With *K$* being a null string ("") and *T* having a value greater than zero.

In the first case, the computer reads the keyboard and if a key is being pressed, the value of the character of that key is assigned to *key$*. If no key is being pressed, the computer does not wait (since *T*=0), and the loop continues. At line 130, *key$*, is tested to see if the key pressed is that specified by *K$*. If so, the loop ends and so does the procedure. If not, the loop is repeated since *T* is equal to zero and the second condition in line 130 is false. In this mode the procedure waits for a specified key.

In the second case described above, there is no need for a key to be pressed because line 120 makes the computer wait only for the specified time before continuing. Then, at line 130, the second condition is true (*T*>0) so the loop and procedure end. If, while waiting, any key is pressed, the computer continues to line 130 and the second condition is true. The loop and procedure end.

Calling program: There are two ways of responding to the calling program, depending on how you want the procedure to operate.
1)   Indefinite wait for a specified key: Press the key you intend to specify when asked (line 20). When asked to specify the time, enter 0.
     The computer waits until you press the key you have specified. Then it displays the message 'FINISHED'.
2)   Wait for any key or a period of time: Do not press any key when asked to specify a key. Simply press RETURN. When asked to specify the time, key in a number equal to the time required, in hundredths of a second (e.g. key 500 for a 5-second wait). The computer displays the 'FINISHED' message as soon as you press any key. If you do not press a key, it displays the message after the specified time has elapsed (e.g. after 5 seconds).

The first way of using the procedure is useful when it is important for the user to press a particular key before the program can continue. For example, to press 'R' to indicate that the tape recorder is set up ready for loading data. The second way of using the procedure is useful when, for example, the user is being asked to read a screenful of text. The waiting period is set long enough to give a slow reader time to read the text. Then the program continues. But a fast reader, or a user who has read the text before, can press any key to make the program continue without further delay.
    The procedure may be used for both purposes in the same program simply by calling it with appropriate parameters.

Associated routines: PROCdelay.

PROCwarning

What it does: Produces a warbling warning sound.

Formal parameters: None.

Local variables: None.

Actual parameters: None.

Listing:

```
10 PROCwarning
20 END
30 REM *************************
40 DEF PROCwarning
50 ENVELOPE 1,2,1,0,0,15,0,0,126,0,0,
-126,126,126
60 SOUND 1,1,150,254
70 ENDPROC
```

How it works: Line 50 defines ENVELOPE 1 with a very short step length (2). The parameters 1,0,0 produce a slowly rising pitch in section 1. The parameters 15,0,0 make section 1 fifteen steps long, and there are no second and third phases. The overall effect of the pitch parameters is to produce a regular and repeated sequence of rising notes, creating an insistent warbling effect. Attack is at maximum rate (126), so the sound begins at maximum volume. Amplitude is held constant during the decay and sustain phases (0,0). It falls sharply (−126) during the release phase. Target levels are set high (126,126) to maintain maximum volume.

The SOUND statement at line 60 uses a tone channel (channel 1) and ENVELOPE 1 (just defined). The pitch is fairly high (150) and the duration is just over 12 seconds (254).

Calling program: When the program is run, the procedure is called and the sound is heard. In your own programs it is a good idea to reserve ENVELOPE 1 for this procedure and for any other sound-effects procedures that may be used. Then ENVELOPE 1 is redefined each time one of these procedures is called. The other envelopes may then be defined globally at the beginning of the program to provide for musical tones and tunes.

Variations: To produce a range of different alarm tones (perhaps for giving warnings of different happenings) try altering the pitch of the SOUND command; change the 150 in line 60 to any other value between 0 and 254. Usually the higher-pitched notes (lower values) are more penetrating. If you want the sound to continue indefinitely, instead of lasting for only 12 seconds, change the 254 in line 60 to −1. You can also get different kinds of warning sounds by altering the envelope. Experiment with changing the amount by which pitch rises and falls (e.g. change the 1 to 2 or 4). Also vary the number of steps by which the pitch rises (e.g. alter the 15 to 25 or 50).

Section 2
Functions

Functions and how they work

The definition of a function begins by stating its name and by listing the variables it is to operate on. For example, if we are writing a function to take the value of the cube of a number, we might begin:

    500 DEF FNcube(N)

The variable in brackets after the function name is called the *argument* of the function. It is similar to a parameter, as was used in the definition of a procedure (see Section 1). In practice, many people refer to it as a parameter, since it is simpler to use the same name for something that has more or less the same effect. The difference between a parameter and an argument stems from the difference between procedures and functions. Procedures *do* things and usually need parameters to control their actions (e.g. exactly where on the screen to display a given message, or how long to wait for a key-press). They *use* the parameters but do not necessarily do anything to them.

The sole purpose of a function is to take the argument and tell us what value is obtained when it has worked on it in a given way. FNcube for example, given the argument 3, tells us that 3 cubed produces the result 27.

Having said what FNcube does, let us look at its listing:

    500 DEF FNcube(N)
    510 =N*N*N

There is no such word as ENDFN to end the definition of a function. Instead we finish it with an equals sign, followed by a variable or expression which gives a value to the function. Many functions are simple, one-line definitions (excluding the name and parameter), though some functions are much more complicated. There may be several lines of calculation, perhaps involving other functions before the final equals sign is reached.

Calling a function is not quite the same thing as calling a procedure.

Perhaps it is more helpful to refer to the action as *using* a function. With a procedure we think of the computer as being sent off to some other part of the program to carry out a set of instructions and (when it reaches ENDPROC) to return to the point at which it was called and continue with the next instruction. But a function call is often embedded in a complicated expression. The computer goes off in the middle of working out the value of the expression to evaluate the function, then returns (having reached the =) and continues with its calculations. For example, when we use an expression such as

$$L = SIN(A)*X + 250$$

we know that the computer goes to a machine-code routine in its monitor program to evaluate the function SIN(A), but we do not normally refer to this as 'calling the SIN function'. Similarly, FNcube, or any other function we may define for ourselves in the BASIC program, is *used*, rather than called. Thinking of it in this way helps to emphasise the difference between procedures and functions and also helps to ensure that we use them correctly.

The function above has one argument, but there may be more than one if required. For example, FNroundednumber (described in this section) has two arguments. This function takes a number and rounds it off to any chosen number of decimal places. The first of its arguments is the number which is to be rounded, while the second is the number of decimal places required.

Functions may operate on strings too. We already have several examples in BASIC – LEFT$, RIGHT$, and MID$ are string functions, and their values are strings. The function LEN, on the other hand, takes a string as its argument but its value is a number.

As with the parameters of procedures, the arguments of functions are either *formal* or *actual*. Formal arguments are local, as are any variables defined by LOCAL within the function. For a further discussion of these terms, see Section 1. The discussion on how to link procedures to your programs, using your own variable names, values or expressions as parameters also applies to arguments of functions.

Describing the functions

In the section of the book which follows, each function is described under the following headings:

What it does: a brief description of its action.

Formal arguments: a list of the variables, in order of appearance in the procedure, and how they are used.

Local variables: a list of the variables and how they are used.

Actual arguments: a list of the values, variables or expressions.

Global arrays: a list of these (if any) and how they are used.

Listing: this is in two parts – an example of a calling program, followed by the function. The listing has a line of asterisks to make it easier to distinguish one part from the other.

How it works: a description of the operation of the function.

Calling program: a brief description of how to use this. This program is intended to show you how to use the function in your own program. It is normally designed so that you can feed a range of values to the function and find out what result is obtained.

Variations: ways to modify the function to make it perform in other ways.

Associated routines: cross references to procedures or other functions which have actions related to that of the function.

The Functions

FNacceptletter

What it does: Waits for the user to key in a letter or numeral that belongs to a specified set. On return, the value of the function is the accepted letter or numeral.

Formal arguments: *L$*, a string made up of the acceptable letters or numerals.

Local variables: *key$*, the letter or numeral that is keyed in by the user.

Actual arguments: *letter$*.

Listing:

```
 10 CLS
 20 INPUT "Range of acceptable letters
"letter$
 30 PRINT "Select a letter "
 40 PRINT FNacceptletter(letter$)
 50 END
 60 REM ***********************
 70 DEF FNacceptletter(L$)
 80 LOCAL key$
 90 REPEAT:key$=GET$
100   UNTIL INSTR(L$,key$)
110 =key$
```

How it works: The REPEAT ... UNTIL loop of lines 90 to 100 repeatedly accepts key-presses, the letter or numeral being stored in *key$*. INSTR is used to find out if this letter or numeral is included in the acceptable set, held in *L$*. If it is included, the loop ends and the function is given the value of this letter or numeral.

Calling program: You are first asked to key in a string containing the acceptable letters. The program displays the message 'Select a letter' and then calls the function in a PRINT statement (line 40) to wait for your reply. As soon as you key in a letter that is included in the acceptable set, this letter is displayed.

Variations: Here are some examples of strings that may be used for *letter$* in your own programs. If the function is to be used to accept the reply to a question which has to be answered with a yes or no, a suitable string is "YN". However, if it is possible that the user may type the reply in lower-case, the string should by "YyNn". In choosing from a menu of items identified by letters from A to F, the string should be "ABCDEF". Alternatively, numerals may be used for menu selection, for example "01234". If you require the user to type in a single-digit integer value within a given range, use a string such as "34567". The numeric value of the entry can be assigned to a variable by a statement such as X=FNacceptletter ("34567").

Associated routines: PROCselectanumber.

FNaccumulator

What it does: Reads the content of the accumulator register of the computer's microprocessor.

Formal arguments: None.

Local variables: None.

Actual arguments: None.

Global arrays: *CODE%*, required for the assembler routine.

Listing:

```
10 CLS
20 DIM CODE% 0
30 P%=CODE%
40 [ OPT 0
50 RTS
60 ]
70 INPUT "VALUE "A%
80 PRINT "ACCUMULATOR CONTAINS ";→FNa
ccumulator
```

```
 90 END
100 REM ***********************
110 DEF FNaccumulator
120 =USR(CODE%)AND&FF
```

The right-arrow (→) in line 80 represents the ~ character on the BBC Micro's keyboard.

How it works: The USR function calls the machine code routine and returns with a value related to the contents of the Y and X registers and the accumulator. Expressed as a 6-digit hexadecimal number this has the format YYXXAA, in which YY represents the content of the Y register, etc. The content of the accumulator is extracted from this number by ANDing it with &FF.

Calling program: This begins by dimensioning a 1-byte block of memory to hold the machine code routine. Next comes a short assembler routine – the shortest possible, since it just tells the microprocessor to return to the main program. The purpose of this routine is simply to set up the conditions needed for USR. If you are using FNxregister and FNyregister in the same program, lines 20 to 60 will do for all three functions.

In trying out this function, input any integer value between −255 and 255. The accumulator cannot hold values outside this range. The resident integer variable, $A\%$, is assigned this value. When the USR call is made, this value is automatically put into the accumulator. Nothing further happens to it, and on return from USR it is represented in the value of USR, as explained above. The value of FNaccumulator is displayed as a hexadecimal value (line 80), since this is the most convenient form.

Note that it is not necessary for the computer to pass through the assembler routine more than once, on the first occasion that a program is RUN. The function may be used any number of times after that.

Variations: Apart from its use in programs, this function can be very helpful when you are developing a program or part of a program in assembler. First of all, delete line 70, since the value will now be put in the accumulator by your own assembler program. Next, alter the DIM in line 20 to allow enough bytes for the program you are writing. Write your assembler program a little at a time by keying in the first few lines of it between lines 40 and 50. You can renumber the program if you need more room. When you reach a stage in the program at which you want to know the value held in the accumulator, run the calling program. The computer will assemble your routine. Then the function is called. This first causes the computer to carry out the assembled machine code instructions and then it returns to BASIC and displays the content of the accumulator. If all is as expected, add more lines to the assembler, then re-run the calling program to test the lines added. Note that you can use OPT 1, 2, or 3 in line 40, if you would like an assembler listing and an error report.

Associated routines: FNxregister, FNyregister.

FNanagram

What it does: Produces an anagram of a word (i.e. a *scrambled* word).

Formal arguments: *W$*, the word.

Local variables: *J*, loop index.
number, a randomly selected number.
flag, a flag, which is true (i.e. equal to -1) if the value of *number* has been selected previously.
anagran $, the string in which the anagram is built up.

Actual arguments: *word$*.

Global arrays: *position*, stores the sequence of randomly selected numbers.

Listing:

```
 10 CLS
 20 DIM position(10)
 30 INPUT "Enter the word "word$
 40 PRINT "The anagram is - "FNanagram
(word$)
 50 END
 60 REM ***********************
```

```
  70 DEF FNanagram(W$)
  80 LOCAL J,number,flag,anagram$
  90 FOR J=1 TO LEN(W$)
 100    number=RND(LEN(W$))
 110    IF J=1 THEN 160
 120    flag=FALSE:FOR K=1 TO J-1
 130       IF position(K)=number THEN fla
g=TRUE
 140       NEXT
 150    IF flag THEN 100
 160    position(J)=number
 170    NEXT
 180 FOR J=1 TO LEN(W$)
 190    anagram$=anagram$+MID$(W$,positi
on(J),1)
 200    NEXT
 210 =anagram$
```

How it works: Rather than try to scramble the letters of the word, we scramble the numbers which represents the positions of the letters in the word. For example, if the word is LOOPED, the letters and their positions are:

L O O P E D
1 2 3 4 5 6

Now we scramble the positions to give, for example:

4 3 2 6 1 5
P O O D L E

The function operates by selecting random numbers (between 1 and the number of letters in the word), making sure that no number is selected twice. Then the anagram is assembled by picking out the letters from the original word, in the order specified by the numbers.

The loop at line 90 to 170 selects the random numbers. Line 100 selects a number. On the first time through the loop *J* equals 1, so line 110 sends the computer directly to line 160. Here the number is stored as the first value in *position*(). From now on it is essential that no number is selected more than once. The loop repeats and a new number is selected. This time through the loop, and on all subsequent repetitions of the loop, the computer goes to the loop in lines 120 to 140. Before starting this loop, *flag* is made false (i.e. equal to 0). Then the loop compares the current value of *number* with all of the values already stored in *position()* so far. If a value is found that equals *number, flag* is made true. As soon as the loop is finished, line 150 tests to see if *flag* is true (i.e. if the current value of *number* has already been picked). If so, the computer is sent back to line 100 to select another value for *number*. If *flag* is false, the computer continues to line 160 where it stores the new random value in *position*(). The loop repeats, selecting yet another number until *position*() has a number for each letter of *word$*.

The loop at lines 180 to 200 builds up *anagram$* character by character. The letters are picked from *word$* by using the values stored in *position*(). Since no two numbers are repeated, every letter or *word$* is used and the result is an anagram. The function is assigned the value of *anagram$* at line 210.

Calling program: The program dimensions the array at line 20, to hold ten letters. If you want to make anagrams of words longer than ten letters, increase the '10' in line 20. You are asked to type in the word in line 30 and line 40 uses FNanagram to find an anagram and display it.

Variations: It is interesting to add to the program. For example, putting line 40 into a FOR ... NEXT loop, displays a dozen or more anagrams of the word.

The main purpose of this function is for producing anagrams for puzzle games. However, the routines of lines 90 to 170 have more serious uses in statistical programs. They produce random assortments of numbers, (but only one of each value), which can be used in Monte Carlo methods for estimating probabilities in distribution-free tests (see Bishop and Bishop, *Figuring Out Facts*, published in this series by Granada).

FNbase

What it does: Returns a given number expressed to any required base.

Formal arguments: N, the number.
  B, the required base.

Local variables: *power*, the power to which B is raised.
  result$, a string in which the converted number is built up.
  digit, takes the value of each digit of the converted number, expressed in decimal.

code, the ASCII code of the character corresponding to *digit*.

Actual arguments: *number*, *base*.

Listing:

```
10 CLS
20 INPUT "Number "number
30 INPUT "Base "base
40 PRINT;number;" to base ";base;" is
".;FNbase(number,base)
50 END
60 REM *************************
70 DEF FNbase(N,B)
80 LOCAL power,result$,digit,code
90 REPEAT power=power+1
100    UNTIL B↑power>N
110 power=power-1
120 REPEAT digit=N/B↑power
130    IF digit<1 THEN result$=result$+
"0":GOTO 170
140    code=48+digit:IF code>57 THEN co
de=code+7
150    result$=result$+CHR$(code)
160    N=N-INT(digit)*B↑power
170    power=power-1
180    UNTIL power=-1
190 =result$
```

How it works: The function consists of two REPEAT ... UNTIL loops. In the first loop, *power* is increased from zero in steps of 1 until B to the power *power* is greater than N. *Power* is then decremented by 1. This finds the largest power of B which can be divided into N to give a result greater than 1.

The second loop begins by dividing N by B to find the value of the first digit. On the first time round the loop this is bound to be greater than 1. It could have any value from 1 to $B-1$. In a hexadecimal convertion, for example, B is 16 and *digit* could have any value from 1 to 16. In building up the converted number we have to replace any two-digit decimal number by a single digit. Line 140 finds the ASCII code of the corresponding alphanumeric character. If *digit* is between 1 and 9, *code* takes a value corresponding to the characters 0 to 9. If *digit* is greater than 9, *code* takes values corresponding to the letters of the alphabet from A onwards. With a large base, the alphabet may have insufficient letters. The symbols [, \,], ^, −, and £ are used next, followed by the lower-case alphabet. Finally we use {, ¦, }, and ~. In all, 72 characters are available, allowing numbers up to base 73 to be converted.

As the ASCII code for each digit is obtained, the corresponding character is added to *result$* (line 150). The decimal value of that digit is then subtracted from *N* and *power* is decremented by 1. This operation is repeated to obtain the next digit, until *power* has been reduced to zero. It may happen that the value of *N* at a given stage is less than *B* to the power *power*. In this event *digit* is less than 1 (line 130). A zero is put into *result$* and *power* is reduced by 1 before the loop is repeated. The converted number is gradually built up in *result$* and this determines the value of the function (line 190).

Calling program: You are asked to key in the number and the base, after which the value of the function is displayed.

FNcombinations

What it does: Calculates the number of ways of selecting a group of a given size from a given number of objects or individuals. Mathematically, this is expressed as $_nC_r$.

Formal arguments: *N*, the total number of objects or individuals from which the selection is made.
   R, the number of objects or individuals in a group.

Local variables: None.

Actual arguments: *total*, *group*.

Listing:

```
10 CLS
20 INPUT "Total number "total
30 INPUT "Number in each group "group
40 PRINT "The number of combinations
is "iFNcombinations(total,group)
50 END
60 DEF FNfactoriallow(N)
```

```
  70 IF N=0 THEN =1
  80 LOCAL fact,J
  90 fact=1
 100 FOR J=1 TO N:fact=fact*J:NEXT
 110 =fact
 120 REM ************************
 130 DEF FNcombinations(N,R)
 140 =INT(FNfactoriallow(N)/FNfactorial
low(R)/FNfactoriallow(N-R))
```

How it works: The function calculates the number of combinations by using the equation:

$$_nC_r = \frac{N!}{R!(N-R)!}$$

It requires a function (FNfactoriallow) to evaluate the factorials.

Calling program: The total and the number in a group are input and sent directly to the function. The calling program includes FNfactoriallow, which FNcombinations uses for evaluating the factorials. If the value of N or R may exceed 33, use FNfactorialhigh instead of FNfactoriallow.

Associated routines: FNfactoriallow, FNfactorialhigh.

FNdeek

What it does: Returns a value (0–65536) stored in two consecutive bytes of memory.

Formal arguments: A, the first of the two memory addresses.

Local variables: None.

Actual arguments: *address.*

Listing:

```
  10 CLS
  20 INPUT "Base address (HEX) "address
$
```

```
30 address=EVAL("&"+address$)
40 PRINT "Content = ";FNdeek(address)
50 END
60 REM **********************************
70 DEF FNdeek(A)
80 =?A+256*A?1
```

How it works: This routine assumes that the value is stored in the conventional way, the low byte being followed by the high byte. It uses the indirection operator (?) to read the value of the low byte (at A) and then reads the high byte (at $A+1$), which is multiplied by 256 before being added to the low byte. The total is returned as the value of the function.

Calling program: Since addresses are more commonly expressed in hexadecimal, the calling program allows you to key in the address in this form. The input accepts the address as a string, *address$*. This has "&" added to it so that it is recognisable by the computer as a hexadecimal number (line 30) and this becomes the value of *address*.
   This function can be used to read data which you have previously stored in blocks of memory, or for reading double-byte values stored by the computer. For example, try reading &352 and &353 (key in 352 only). This pair of bytes stores the number of bytes taken per character row of the screen. Change mode, then use the function to read these two bytes again.

Associated routines: PROCdoke.

FNdifferentiate

What it does: Returns, in the form of a string, an expression equal to the differential of a given expression.

Formal arguments: $Y\$$, the expression to be differentiated, in string form.
   $X\$$, the variable with respect to which the expression is to be differentiated.

Local variables: E, the position of the ^ within $Y\$$.

Actual arguments: *exp$*, *diff$*.

Listing:

```
10 CLS
20 INPUT "y = "exp$
30 INPUT "Differentiate with respect
to "diff$
40 PRINT "dy/dx = ";FNdifferentiate(e
xp$,diff$)
50 END
60 REM *************************
70 DEF FNdifferentiate(Y$,X$)
80 LOCAL E
90 IF INSTR(Y$,X$)=0 THEN ="0"
100 IF INSTR(Y$,"↑")=0 THEN Y$=Y$+"↑1"
110 E=INSTR(Y$,"↑")
120 =RIGHT$(Y$,LEN(Y$)-E)+"*"+LEFT$(Y$
,E-1)+"↑"+STR$(VAL(RIGHT$(Y$,LEN(Y$)-E))
-1)
```

How it works: The function requires the expression to be in the form:

constant*variable^exponent

Examples are $3*X^4$, $5.6*X^7$. The constant and the exponent may be negative and need not be integers. Expressions such as:

$$\frac{3}{X^5}$$

should be presented as:

$3*X^{-5}$

The variable may be any single letter. The constant may consist of several constants with multiplication or division signs between them. The constant may include one or more variable names *that have already been used* in the main program. (Example, $.5*mass*V^2$, where *V* is the variable).

Given an expression in the above format, the function searches it to find if the variable is present (line 90). If not, the expression as a whole is a constant and when differentiated, gives zero.

Next the function searches for the exponentiation operator (line 100). If this is absent, it is assumed that the expression is one such as

4*X, in which the $\wedge$ 1 is 'understood'. This missing $\wedge$ is then added to Y$. The position of the $\wedge$ within the string is determined in line 110. Finally, the function constructs a string, using the relationship:

$$\frac{d(a.x^{h})}{dy} = b.a.x^{(h-1)}$$

The routine does simplify the expression (i.e. by multiplying constants together), but its final form is such that it can readily be evaluated.

Calling program: The program asks you to type in the expression, which must be in the format described above. It then asks with respect to which variable the differentiantion is to be performed. Key in a single letter. These two strings are then passed to the function, and the result displayed.

Variations: The function may use itself to calculate the second differential (d^2x/dy^2) of the expression. The value required is:

FNdifferentiate(FNdifferentiate(exp$,diff$),diff$).

Associate routines: FNvaldifferentiate.

FNfactorialhigh

What it does: Calculates the factorial of any number.

Formal arguments: *N*, the number to be factorialised.

Local variables: *fact*, the factorial.
  J, the loop index.

Actual arguments: *number*.

Listing:

```
10 CLS
20 INPUT "NUMBER (>=0) "number
30 PRINT "Factorial "inumberi" is "iF
Nfactorialhigh(number)
40 END
```

```
 50  REM  *************************
 60  DEF  FNfactorialhigh(N)
 70  IF  N=0  THEN  =1
 80  LOCAL  fact,J
 90  fact=0
100  FOR  J=1  TO  N:fact=fact+LOG(J):NEXT

110  =STR$(10^(fact-INT(fact)))+"E"+STR
$(INT(fact))
```

How it works: This function allows very large factorials to be calculated. Instead of multiplying values together (see FNfactoriallow), it adds their logarithms. With large numbers this inevitably leads to loss of precision so, if you know that you will not need to calculate factorials of numbers greater than 33, it is much better to use FNfactoriallow.

The loop is repeated *N* times. The initial value of *fact* is 0 and it has the logarithm of *J* added to it each time round the loop. If *N* is 6, for example, *J* increases in steps of 1 from 1 to 6. The result is that *fact* becomes the sum of logarithms of integers from 1 to 6. It is not possible to use EXP to convert this result to the factorial because the result is likely to be too large. Instead, line 110 builds up a string to express the factorial in the standard exponential form. The value of factorial zero (0!) is 1; line 70 provides for this.

Calling program: This simply accepts any number as an input and sends it to the function, the value of which is displayed. Numbers should be positive integers. The larger the number, the longer it takes to calculate the factorial. We have not discovered which is the largest possible number this routine can factorialise, nor the precision of the values of very large factorials.

Associated routines: FNfactoriallow.

FNfactoriallow

What it does: Calculates the factorial of any number from 0 to 33.

Formal arguments: *N*, the number to be factorialised.

Local variables: *fact*, the factorial.
   J, the loop index.

Actual arguments: *number*.

Listing:

```
 10 CLS
 20 INPUT "NUMBER (0-33) "number
 30 PRINT "Factorial ";number;" is ";F
Nfactoriallow(number)
 40 END
 50 REM *************************
 60 DEF FNfactoriallow(N)
 70 IF N=0 THEN =1
 80 LOCAL fact,J
 90 fact=1
100 FOR J=1 TO N:fact=fact*J:NEXT
110 =fact
```

How it works: The loop is repeated N times. The initial value of *fact* is 1, and it is multiplied by J each time round the loop. If N is 6, for example, J increases in steps of 1 from 1 to 6. The result is that *fact* = 1 $\times 2 \times 3 \times 4 \times 5 \times 6$; in other words, it becomes factorial 6 (6!). The value of factorial zero (0!) is 1; line 70 provides for this.

Calling program: This simply accepts any number as an input and sends it to the function, the value of which is displayed. Numbers should be integers between 0 and 33. Numbers larger than 33 produce a result which is too large for the computer to handle.

Associated routines: FNfactorialhigh.

FNformstring

What it does: Pads out a string with spaces to give it a specified length.

Formal arguments: *T$*, the string.
   L, the required length.

Local variables: *J*, loop index.
   textlength, the length of the string before padding.

Actual arguments: *text$, length.*

Listing:

```
  10 CLS
  20 INPUT "Length of padded string "le
ngth
  30 INPUT "Text to be entered "text$
  40 PRINT FNformstring(text$,length);"
<----";
  50 PRINT "This is the padded string"
  60 END
  70 REM ***************************
  80 DEF FNformstring(T$,L)
  90 LOCAL J,textlength
 100 textlength=LEN(T$)
 110 FOR J=1 TO (L-textlength)
 120   T$=T$+" "
 130   NEXT J
 140 =LEFT$(T$,L)
```

How it works: Line 100 assigns the original length of the string to 'textlength'. The loop in lines 110 to 130 adds as many spaces to the string as are needed to pad it out to the required length. This assumes that the string was less than the required length to begin with. In any event, the loop always adds one space to the string, since the instructions in a loop are always carried out at least once. For these reasons, the string may possibly be longer than the specified length. At line 140, the function is assigned the value of the first L characters of T, so reducing an overlong string to the required length.

Calling program: Key in the required length of the string (line 20). Then enter the text. As explained above, this may be longer than the required length, in which case it will be chopped down to size. As soon as you have keyed in the text, the function is displayed. An arrow and the message 'This is the padded string' is displayed immediately to the right of the padded string, with no spaces between. This is to let you see the spaces which have been added by the function.

FNfree

What it does: Finds how much user memory is free.

Formal arguments: None.

Local variables: None.

Actual arguments: None.

Listing:

```
10 CLS
20 PRINT "BYTES FREE = ";FNfree
30 END
40 REM ************************
50 DEF FNfree
60 =(?5-?3)*256+?4-?2
```

How it works: Two bytes in RAM (addresses 4 and 5) hold the lowest address of the BASIC stack. This sets the upper limit of memory available to the user. Two other bytes (addresses 2 and 3) hold the highest address of the variable storage area, which sets the lower limit of available memory. The function calculates the difference between these two values, giving the number of free bytes available.

Calling program: Line 20 displays the message 'BYTES FREE =' and the function provides the required number.

FNhcf

What it does: Finds the highest common factor of any two positive integers.

Formal arguments: $X\%$ and $Y\%$, the two integers.

Local variables: None.

Actual arguments: *first%, second%.*

Listing:

```
 10 CLS
 20 INPUT "First value "first%
 30 INPUT "Second value "second%
 40 PRINT "HCF = ";FNhcf(first%,second%)
 50 END
 60 REM ***********************
 70 DEF FNhcf(X%,Y%)
 80 IF X%>Y% THEN X%=X%-Y%
 90 IF X%<Y% THEN Y%=Y%-X%
100 IF X%<>Y% THEN 80
110 =X%
```

How it works: This makes use of Euclid's algorithm for finding the highest common factor.

Calling program: The two numbers are keyed in and immediately used when the function is displayed at line 40.

FNjoystick

What it does: Returns a message string indicating the state of the joystick.

Formal arguments: N, the number of the joystick.

Local variables: *stick*, the reading from the analogue-to-digital converter.
LR$, the string indicating left-right positions.
UD$, the string indicating up-down positions (i.e. upwards and downwards on the screen).
fire$, the string indicating if the fire button is being pressed.

Actual arguments: *joystick*.

Listing:

```
 10 CLS
 20 INPUT "Which joystick (1-2) "joyst
ick
 30 FOR J = 1 TO 100
```

```
   40    PRINT "Joystick ";joystick;" is
 ";FNjoystick(joystick)
   50    FOR K =1 TO 500:NEXT
   60    NEXT
   70  END
   80  REM ***************************
   90  DEF FNjoystick(N)
  100  LOCAL stick,LR$,UD$,fire$
  110  stick=ADVAL(0)AND2↑(N-1)
  120  IF stick>0 THEN fire$="firing"
  130  stick=ADVAL(2*N-1)
  140  IF stick>50000 THEN LR$="left "
  150  IF stick<20000 THEN LR$="right "
  160  stick=ADVAL(N*2)
  170  IF stick>50000 THEN UD$="up "
  180  IF stick<20000 THEN UD$="down "
  190  IFLR$="" AND UD$="" THEN LR$="cent
 ered "
  200  =LR$+UD$+fire$
```

How it works: Line 110 reads the output from the A-to-D converter, using ADVAL(0). The state of the bit which indicates whether the button of the selected joystick is being pressed is read by the ANDing operation in that line. If the button is being pressed, *stick* has a value of 1 or 2 (depending on whether joystick 1 or 2 is being read); if the button is not being pressed, *stick* is zero. If the button is being pressed, *fire$* is given the value "firing" (in line 120).

In line 130, *stick* is given the value of ADVAL(1), for joystick 1 or ADVAL(3), for joystick 2. This has a value ranging from 0 if the stick is to the far right, to 65520 if the stick is to the far left. Lines 140 and 150 give appropriate values to *LR$* if the value of *stick* lies toward either end of the range.

A similar routine is followed in lines 160 to 180, with respect to ADVAL(2) or ADVAL(4), to determine the value of *UD$*.

If, at line 190, both *LR$* and *UD$* are null strings, this must be because the joystick is near its central position. If so, *LR$* is given the value "centred".

Finally, FNjoystick is given the value of the three strings concatenated together, in line 200.

Calling program: Before running this program, plug one or two proportional joysticks into the analogue socket of the computer. Then run the program. You are asked to specify which joystick is to be read. The program reads the joystick 100 times, with a slight delay (line 50) between each reading. It displays FNjoystick to show each of the readings and a succession of messages scroll up the screen. While this is happening, move the joystick and occasionally press the fire button. The messages change accordingly. Examples of messages you will see are 'centred', 'left', 'left firing', 'right down', 'right up firing' and so on. When the display ceases, you can begin again, using the same joystick or the other one.

Variations: The messages could be displayed on the screen to indicate the action of a game. You can quite easily change the exact wording to suit the game or other application. This function could be used for an entirely different purpose, such as allowing input to the computer of a limited range of words or commands without the keyboard. A disabled person could communicate with the computer to a limited extent by using this function.

If the function is being used simply to control the computer, and not for displaying the messages, the messages could be shortened to single letters, or even replaced by numerical values. The joystick could control the operation of a program, using lines such as:

        IF FNjoystick(1)="A" THEN 500

or

        IF FNjoystick(2)=5 THEN 1000

There are many other possible applications for this function.

FNlimit

What it does: Holds a given value between pre-set lower and upper limits.

Formal arguments: *V*, the value to be held.
  L, the lower limit.
  U, the upper limit.

Local variables: None.

Actual arguments: *value, lower, upper.*

Listing:

```
  10 CLS
  20 INPUT "Lower limit "lower
  30 INPUT "Upper limit "upper
  40 INPUT "Value "value
  50 PRINT "Limited value is ";FNlimit(
value,lower,upper)
  60 END
  70 REM ************************
  80 DEF FNlimit(V,L,U)
  90 IF V<L THEN =L
 100 IF V>U THEN =U
 110 =V
```

How it works: If V is below the lower limit (line 90), or above the upper limit (line 100), the function is made equal to the limit concerned. Otherwise, the function has the value of V.

Calling program: You can set the lower and upper limits to any values, including negative ones, providing you make the lower limit less than the upper one. You can key in any value. These three numbers are made the actual arguments of the function. Line 50 displays the result.

This function has many applications in games programs in which a graphics character (e.g. a spacecraft) is to be moved about the screen. The calculations within the program, or routines which respond to key-presses or a joystick, produce values used in displaying the character. This function can be used to limit the region of the screen in which the character may be displayed. If TAB(X,Y) is being used, in Mode 4, use FNlimit to hold X between 0 and 39, and to limit Y between 0 and 23. This will prevent the character from moving off the screen and also prevent illegal values being used in the TAB statement.

FNmax

What it does: Finds the maximum of a set of values held in an array.

Formal arguments: None.

Local variables: *max*, the maximum value.
   J, the loop counter.

Actual arguments: None.

Global arrays: *number*, the set of values.

Global variables: *total*, the number of values in *number*(). You can replace this with a constant in your calling program and in the function.

Listing:

```
  10 CLS
  20 INPUT "Enter total numbers "total
  30 DIM number(total)
  40 FOR J=1 TO total
  50    INPUT "Enter a number "number(J)
  60    NEXT
  70 PRINT;FNmax;
  80 PRINT " is the maximum number"
  90 END
 100 REM *************************
 110 DEF FNmax
 120 LOCAL max,J
 130 max=number(1)
 140 FOR J=2 TO total
 150    IF number(J)>max THEN max=number
(J)
 160    NEXT
 170 =max
```

How it works: To begin with (line 130), *max* is assigned the first of the values in *number*(). The loop of lines 140 to 160 compares *max* with the second and subsequent values in *number*(). Whenever a value is found in *number*() that is greater than the current value of *max*, then *max* is assigned that value. The function takes the final value of *max* at line 170.

Calling program: You are first asked how many numbers you want to use to test FNmax. The array is then dimensioned (line 30). Next you are asked to key in a set of numbers to fill the array. This completed, the calling program displays the value of the function.

Associated routines: FNmin.

FNmin

What it does: Finds the minimum of a set of values held in an array.

Formal arguments: None.

Local variables: *min*, the minimum value.
  J, the loop counter.

Actual arguments: None.

Global arrays: *number*, the set of values.

Global variables: *total*, the number of values in *number*(). You can replace this with a constant in your calling program and in the function.

Listing:

```
 10 CLS
 20 INPUT "Enter total numbers "total
 30 DIM number(total)
 40 FOR J=1 TO total
 50   INPUT "Enter a number "number(J)
 60   NEXT
 70 PRINT;FNmin;
 80 PRINT " is the minimum number"
 90 END
100 REM ************************
110 DEF FNmin
120 LOCAL min,J
130 min=number(1)
140 FOR J=2 TO total
150   IF number(J)<min THEN min=number
J)
160   NEXT
170 =min
```

How it works: To begin with (line 130), *min* is assigned the first of the values in *number*(). The loop of lines 140 to 160 compares *min* with the second and subsequent values in *number*(). Whenever a value is found in *number*() that is less than the current value of *min*, then *min* is assigned that value. The function takes the final value of *min* at line 170.

Calling program: You are first asked how many numbers you want to use to test FNmin. The array is then dimensioned (line 30). Next you are asked to key in a set of numbers to fill the array. This completed, the calling program displays the value of the function.

Associated routines: FNmax.

FNroundednumber

What it does: Rounds a given number to a specified number of decimal places.

Formal arguments: *P*, the number of decimal places to which *N* is to be rounded.
    N, the number to be rounded.

Local variables: *power*, the value of 10 to the power *P*.

Actual arguments: *places*, *number*.

Listing:

```
 10 CLS
 20 INPUT "Enter a number "number
 30 INPUT "Enter how many decimal plac
es? "places
 40 PRINT "The rounded number is ";FNr
oundednumber(places,number)
 50 END
 60 REM ************************
 70 DEF FNroundednumber(P,N)
 80 LOCAL power
 90 power=10↑P
100 =INT((N+0.5/power)*power)/power
```

How it works: In order to save the time needed for calculating 10 to the power *P* three times during the rounding routine, *power* is assigned this

this value in line 90. Line 100 is a version of the standard algorithm for rounding.

Calling program: You are asked to key in the number to be rounded and to how many decimal places it is to be rounded. Line 40 then prints the value of the function.

FNscreencharacter

What it does: Reads screen memory to find which character is displayed in any given screen location.

Formal arguments: *X*, *Y*, the TAB values for the positions being read.

Local variables: *A%*, resident integer variable, for indicating the OSBYTE call.
horizontal, horizontal positions of the cursor when the function is called.
vertical, vertical position of the cursor when the function is called.
character, the ASCII code of the character.

Listing:

```
 10 MODE 4
 20 VDU 23,68,196,71,69,127,124,124,72
,108
 30 INPUT "Enter a letter "letter$
 40 INPUT "Enter the X coordinate "tab
x
 50 INPUT "Enter the Y coordinate "tab
y
 60 CLS
 70 PRINT TAB(tabx,taby)letter$
 80 char=FNscreencharacter(tabx,taby)
 90 PRINT TAB(tabx+1,taby);"=";char
100 END
110 REM ***********************
120 DEF FNscreencharacter(X,Y)
130 LOCAL A%,horizontal,vertical,chara
cter
```

```
   140  A%=135:horizontal=POS:vertical=VPO
S
   150  VDU 30,31,X,Y
   160  character=(USR(&FFF4)AND&FF00)DIV&
100
   170  VDU 30,31,horizontal,vertical
   180  =character
```

How it works: In line 140, *A%* is given the value 135 (&87), so that the routine for reading the character at the text cursor position will be called by USR in line 160. The remainder of line 140 registers the current position of the cursor, ready for restoring it to that position at line 170, before leaving the function. Line 150 homes the cursor and then positions it at the screen location which is to be read.

In line 160, USR calls the OSBYTE routine and returns from this with the ASCII code for the character in the X register of the microprocessor. The expression in line 160 extracts this value and assigns it to *character*. After restoring the cursor to its original position (line 150), the function is assigned the value of *character* at line 180.

Calling program: The function works in any mode, but line 20 of the calling program is not applicable to Mode 7. Lines 30 to 40, ask you to choose a letter (or any other keyboard character) and say where it is to be displayed on the screen. Line 70 displays the character as requested. The function is now used to read that location on the screen, identify the character and take the value of its ASCII code. The value of the function is then assigned to *char*. Line 90 continues with the display, by placing an equals sign to the right of the character and then printing the value of *char* beside it. If you have keyed 'A', for example, you will see 'A=65' in the chosen position.

The routine works just as well with keyboard characters which have been redefined. If you are in a graphics mode and key 'D' when asked to enter a letter, a picture of a dog appears instead of the letter. This is because line 20 has redefined "D" as a dog character. The program displays the dog in the chosen location. The function finds it and identifies it by the ASCII code for "D" (68). The function is not able to identify user-defined graphics with codes in the range 224–255.

FNvaldifferential

What it does: Evaluates the differential of an expression that is in string form.

Formal arguments: *Y$*, the expression to be differentiated.

X$, the variable with respect to which the expression is to be differentiated.

X, the value of the variable in *X$*.

Local variables: *J*, the loop index.

Actual arguments: *exp$*, *diff$*, *valdiff*.

Listing:

```
  10 CLS
  20 INPUT "y = "exp$
  30 INPUT "Differentiate with respect
to "diff$
  40 PRINT "Value of "diff$;:INPUT "= "
valdiff
  50 PRINT "Value of dy/dx = ";FNvaldif
ferential(exp$,diff$,valdiff)
  60 END
  70 DEF FNdifferentiate(Y$,X$)
  80 LOCAL E
  90 IF INSTR(Y$,X$)=0 THEN ="0"
 100 IF INSTR(Y$,"↑")=0 THEN Y$=Y$+"↑1"
 110 E=INSTR(Y$,"↑")
 120 =RIGHT$(Y$,LEN(Y$)-E)+"*"+LEFT$(Y$
,E-1)+"↑"+STR$(VAL(RIGHT$(Y$,LEN(Y$)-E))
-1)
 130 REM ************************
 140 DEF FNvaldifferential(Y$,X$,X)
 150 LOCAL J
 160 FOR J=1 TO LEN(Y$):IF MID$(Y$,J,1)
=X$ THEN Y$=LEFT$(Y$,J-1)+"X"+RIGHT$(Y$,
LEN(Y$)-J)
 170    NEXT
 180 =EVAL(FNdifferentiate(Y$,"X"))
```

How it works: The function searches $Y\$$ for every occurence of the named variable, $X\$$, and replaces it with X. It then uses FNdifferentiate to differentiate $Y\$$ with respect to X. This call is made within the EVAL function, so that the differentiated expression is evaluated and returned as the value of FNvaldifferential.

Calling program: This asks you to input the expression to be differentiated, the variable with respect to which it is to be differentiated, and the value to be given to this variable when evaluating the differential. The expression must be in the required form (see FNdifferential for a description of this). The program then displays the value of the differential.

The calling program includes FNdifferentiate, which is required by FNvaldifferential.

Variations: This function can be adapted to evaluate the second differential by replacing the expression in EVAL (line 180) by:

FNdifferentiate(FNdifferentiate(exp$,diff$),diff$)

Associated routines: FNdifferentiate.

FNvaliddate

What it does: Validates a date (except 29 February in leap years).

Formal arguments: $D\$$, the date, in the format DDMMYY.

Local variables: *month*, the number of the month.
day, the number of the day in the month.
F, a flag which equals 1 if a non-digit is included in the date.
J, the loop index.
add$, a string of 12 digits representing the number of days additional to the 28 that occur in each of the months.

Actual arguments: *date$*.

Listing:

```
10 CLS
20 REPEAT
```

```
 30    INPUT "DATE-DDMMYY "date$
 40    UNTIL FNvaliddate(date$)
 50  PRINT "O.K."
 60  END
 70  REM *************************
 80  DEF FNvaliddate(D$)
 90  LOCAL month,day,F,J,add$
100  IF LEN D$<>6 THEN=FALSE
110  F=0:FOR J=1 TO 6
120    IF ASC(MID$(D$,J,1))<48 OR ASC(M
ID$(D$,J,1))>57 THEN F=1
130    NEXT
140  month=VAL(MID$(D$,3,2))
150  day=VAL(LEFT$(D$,2))
160  IF F=1 THEN=FALSE
170  IF month<1 OR month>12 THEN=FALSE
180  add$="303232332323"
190  IF day<1 OR day>28+VAL(MID$(add$,m
onth,1)) THEN=FALSE ELSE=TRUE
```

How it works: The date string, *D$*, consists of 6 digits. The first pair represents the day of the month and can have any value from "01" to "28", "30" or "31" depending on the month. The next pair of digits represents the month and can have any value from "01" to "12". The final pair represents the year and can have any value from "00" to "99".

Line 100 checks that the string is made up of exactly 6 digits. If not, the function is given the value FALSE and the computer returns to the calling program. The loop in lines 110 to 130 runs through the string to check that every character is a numeric digit. The flag *F* is set to zero to start with. If any one or more of the characters is a non-digit (i.e. its ASCII code is outside the range 48 to 57), *F* takes the value 1. At line 160 the function receives a FALSE value if *F* equals 1. Now the value of *month* and *day* are found by evaluating the first and second pairs of digits from the string (lines 140 and 150). If *month* is outside the range 1 to 12, the function is given the value FALSE. Line 190 tests if *day* is in the correct range from the given month. The lowest acceptable value is 1, for any month. The highest acceptable value is found by adding the value of one of the digits from *add$* to 28. The expression 'MID$(add$, month,1)' picks out the appropriate digit. For example, if the month is April, *month* is 4. The fourth digit in *add$* is 2 indicating that April has 28+2=30 days. If *day* is outside the correct range, the function is given the value FALSE, otherwise it is given the value TRUE.

Calling program: The program has a loop which asks you to input a date. The loop repeats until the function has a TRUE value (line 40); that is to say, until you have keyed in a valid date. When this happens the computer drops out of the loop and displays the message 'O.K.'.

FNvdudeek

What it does: Reads the value of a VDU variable, stored as a double-byte, using OSBYTE &A40.

Formal arguments: *p%* the address of the first of the bytes, in hexadecimal, relative to &300.

Local variables: *A%*, *X%*, the resident integer variables.
   Q%, the value stored in the double-byte.

Actual arguments: *address.*

Listing:

```
   10 INPUT "What VDU address? (HEX) "ad
dress$
   20 address=EVAL("&"+address$)
   30 PRINT FNvdudeek(address)
   40 END
   50 REM ************************
   60 DEF FNvdudeek(p%)
   70 LOCAL A%,X%,Q%
   80 A%=160:X%=p%
   90 Q%=(USR(&FFF4)AND&FFFF00)/&100
  100 =Q%
```

How it works: Line 80 gives *A%* the value 160 (&A0) so that USR will call OSBYTE &A0. *X%* is assigned the value of the address of the first byte, relative to &300. For example, if the first address is &354, *p%* has the value &54.

   In line 90, USR calls the OSBYTE routine and returns with the combined values of the Y and X registers and the accumulator. The Y register holds the high byte of the number being read, while the X register holds the low byte. When expressed as six-digit hexadecimal number, this has the format YYXXAA. The ANDing operation in line 90 picks out the YYXX digits, zeroing those representing the accumulator. Division by &100 removes the last two zeros from the value. Thus *Q%* takes the value stored in the two bytes. This becomes the value of the function in line 100.

Calling program: Key in the relative address when asked, but do not precede it with a &. Line 20 adds the & so that the value you have keyed in is evaluated as a hexadecimal number. Line 30 prints the value of the function, in decimal. If, for example, you key 50, you will be shown the value stored in &350 and &351. This is the address of the top left corner of screen. Run the program in different modes and see how the address varies.

Variations: If you would prefer to have the values displayed in hexadecimal, insert a ~ before the FN in line 30 of the listing.

Associated routines: FNvdupeek.

FNvdupeek

What it does: Reads the value of a VDU variable, stored as a single byte, using OSBYTE &A40.

Formal arguments: *p%*, the address of the byte, in hexadecimal, relative to &300.

Local variables: *A%*, *X%*, the resident integer variables.
  Q%, the value stored in the byte.

Actual arguments: *address.*

Listing:

```
10 INPUT "What VDU address? (HEX) "ad
dress$
20 address=EVAL("&"+address$)
30 PRINT →FNvdupeek(address)
40 END
50 REM ************************
```

```
  60 DEF FNvdupeek.(p%)
  70 LOCAL A%,X%,Q%
  80 A%=160:X%=p%
  90 Q%=(USR(&FFF4)AND&FF00)/&100
 100 =Q%
```

How it works: Line 80 gives $A\%$ the value 160 (&A0) so that USR will call OSBYTE &A0. $X\%$ is assigned the value of the address of the byte, relative to &300. For example, if the address is &354, $p\%$ has the value &54.

In line 90, USR calls the OSBYTE routine and returns with the combined values of the Y and X registers and the accumulator. The X register holds the value of the byte. When expressed as a six-digit hexadecimal number, this has the format YYXXAA. The ANDing operation in line 90 picks out the XX digits, zeroing those representing the Y register and accumulator. Division by &100 removes the last two zeros from the value. Thus $Q\%$ takes the value stored in the byte. This becomes the value of the function in line 100.

Calling program: Key in the relative address when asked, but do not precede it with a &. Line 20 adds the & so that the value you have keyed in is evaluated as a hexadecimal number. Line 30 prints the value of the function, in decimal. If, for example, you key 55, you will be shown the value stored in &355. This is the current screen mode. Run the program in different modes and see how the displayed value varies.

Variations: If you would prefer to have the values displayed in hexadecimal, insert a ~ before the FN in line 30 of the listing.

Associated routines: FNvdudeek.

FNxregister

What it does: Reads the content of the X register of the computer's microprocessor.

Formal arguments: None.

Local variables: None.

Actual arguments: None.

Global arrays: *CODE%*, required for the assembler routine.

Listing:

```
  10 CLS
  20 DIM CODE% 0
  30 P%=CODE%
  40 [ OPT 0
  50 RTS
  60 ]
  70 INPUT "VALUE "X%
  80 PRINT "X REGISTER CONTAINS ";~FNxr
egister
  90 END
 100 REM ****************************
 110 DEF FNxregister
 120 =(USR(CODE%)AND&FF00)/&100
```

The right-arrow (→) in line 80 represents the ~ character on the BBC Micro's keyboard.

How it works: See FNaccumulator. The content of the X register is extracted by ANDing with &FF00 and dividing the result by &100 to remove the final two zeros.

Calling program: See FNaccumulator.

Variations: See FNaccumulator.

Associated routines: FNaccumulator, FNyregister.

FNyesno

What it does: Waits for the user to key in 'Y', 'y', 'N' or 'n' and returns with the value "Y" or "N".

Formal arguments: None.

Local variables: *key$*, the ASCII code of the key pressed.

Actual arguments: None.

Listing:

```
10 CLS
20 PRINT "Do you want to play again?
Y/N"
30 IF FNyesno="Y" THEN PRINT TAB(15,1
1)"QUIZ GAME" ELSE PRINT TAB(13,11)"Game
finished":END
40 END
50 REM ************************
60 DEF FNyesno
70 LOCAL key$
80 REPEAT
90    key$=CHR$(GET AND &DF)
100   UNTIL INSTR("YN",key$)
110 =key$
```

How it works: The REPEAT ... UNTIL loop (lines 80 to 100) waits for a key to be pressed. The value of GET becomes the ASCII code of the pressed key. This is ANDed with &DF (11011111, in binary) to mask out bit 5. This is the bit which distinguishes between upper-case and lower-case letters. If CAPS LOCK is on, or SHIFT is in operation, GET contains the code for an upper-case (capital) letter. Bit 5 is zero for all these letters, so the ASCII code is unaffected by ANDing. However, if CAPS LOCK is off and SHIFT is not in operation, GET contains the code for a lower-case letter. This has 1 as bit 5, which is converted to 0 by the ANDing. The effect is to convert the code for a lower-case letter to the code for the corresponding upper-case letter. Thus the function works, no matter what the state of CAPS LOCK or SHIFT. The computer drops out of the loop as soon as either key 'Y' or 'N' is pressed and the function takes the corresponding value.

Calling program: The calling program gives an example of the use of this function. A question is asked in line 20. This requires the reply 'Yes' or 'No'. The message prompts the user to key either 'Y' or 'N'. Line 30 sends the computer to different parts of the program depending on the value of the function. If it is 'Y', the computer displays the title of the game; the program for the game could be from line 40 onward. If the value of the function is 'N', the computer displays the message 'Game finished' and the program ends.

FNyregister

What it does: Reads the content of the Y register of the computer's microprocessor.

Formal arguments: None.

Local variables: None.

Actual arguments: None.

Global arrays: *CODE%*, required for the assembler routine.

Listing:

```
 10 CLS
 20 DIM CODE% 0
 30 P%=CODE%
 40 [ OPT 0
 50 RTS
 60 ]
 70 INPUT "VALUE "Y%
 80 PRINT "Y REGISTER CONTAINS ";→FNyr
egister
 90 END
100 REM ************************
110 DEF FNyregister
120 =(USR(CODE%)AND&FF0000)/&10000
```

The right-arrow (→) in line 80 represents the ~ character on the BBC Micro's keyboard.

How it works: See FNaccumulator. The content of the Y register is extracted by ANDing with &FF0000 and dividing the result by &10000 to remove the final four zeros.

Calling program: See FNaccumulator.

Variables: See FNaccumulator.

Associated routines: FNaccumulator, FNxregister.

LOCATOR TABLE

Name of Procedure or Function	Procedure or Function	Page number	Maths	Animation	System	Games	Memory	Graphics	Sound	Data Base	Input	Utilities
acceptletter	F	104				●					●	●
accumulator	F	105	●		●							
anagram	F	107				●						
animate	P	16		●		●	●	●				
base	F	109	●		●							
blankline	P	18									●	●
border	P	19						●				●
box	P	21				●				●		●
central	P	23	●			●						●
circle	P	24				●		●				
clearscreen	P	27						●			●	●
combinations	F	111	●									
deek	F	112					●					●
delay	P	29			●						●	
delete	P	30								●		●

Applications

Function	Type	Page
differentiate	F	113
display	P	33
displayinitial	P	35
doke	P	37
doubleheight	P	38
explode	P	40
factorialhigh	F	115
factoriallow	F	116
formstring	F	117
free	F	119
gunfire	P	41
hcf	F	119
insert	P	42
invisible	P	46
joystick	F	120
keys	P	47
limit	F	122
load	P	48
max	F	123
mean	P	50
min	F	125
moveacross	P	51
movedown	P	53
polygon	P	56
quicksortnumber	P	58

Name of Procedure or Function	Procedure or Function	Utilities	Input	Data Base	Sound	Graphics	Memory	Games	System	Animation	Maths	Page number
quicksortword	P	●		●	●			●				60
rectangle	P		●	●		●	●	●	●			62
reset	P		●			●						63
rightwrong	P											65
rotate	P					●						66
roundednumber	F	●				●					●	126
save	P					●	●	●	●			68
screencharacter	F					●	●	●	●			127
scrolldown	P											70
scrollside	P						●		●			72
selectanumber	P	●	●	●	●	●		●			●	74
sideways	P					●					●	75
solidpolygon	P					●						77
solidrectangle	P							●				79
	P			●				●				81

Applications

Name	Type	Page
table	P	82
telescreen	P	85
timer	P	87
travellingtitle	P	89
tune	P	90
underline	P	93
valdifferential	F	129
validdate	F	130
vdudeek	F	132
vdupeek	F	133
wait	P	94
warning	P	96
xregister	F	134
yesno	F	135
yregister	F	137

Procedure and function locator table